Crime
and the Elderly

CRIME
AND THE ELDERLY

An Annotated Bibliography

COMPILED BY
Ron H. Aday

Foreword by Erdman B. Palmore

Bibliographies and Indexes in Gerontology,
Number 8

Greenwood Press
New York • Westport, Connecticut • London

Library of Congress Cataloging-in-Publication Data

Aday, Ron H.
   Crime and the elderly : an annotated bibliography / compiled by
Ron H. Aday.
      p.   cm. — (Bibliographies and indexes in gerontology, ISSN
0743-7560 ; no. 8)
   Includes indexes.
   ISBN 0-313-25470-2 (lib. bdg. : alk. paper)
   1. Aged—United States—Crimes against—Bibliography.   2. Aged
offenders—United States—Bibliography.   I. Title.   II. Series.
Z5703.4.A35A33   1988
[HV6250.4.A34]
016.3628′8′08805—dc19   88-30051

British Library Cataloguing in Publication Data is available.

Library of Congress Catalog Card Number: 88-30051
ISBN: 0-313-25470-2
ISSN: 0743-7560

First published in 1988

Greenwood Press, Inc.
88 Post Road West, Westport, Connecticut 06881

Printed in the United States of America

The paper used in this book complies with the
Permanent Paper Standard issued by the National
Information Standards Organization (Z39.48-1984).

10 9 8 7 6 5 4 3 2 1

CONTENTS

FOREWORD

The annotated bibliographies in this series provide answers to the fundamental question, "What is known?" Their purpose is simple, yet profound: to provide comprehensive reviews and references for the work done in various fields of gerontology. They are based on the fact that it is no longer possible for anyone to comprehend the vast body of research and writing in even one sub-specialty without years of work.

This fact has become true only in recent years. When I was an undergraduate (Class of '52) I think no one at Duke had even heard of gerontology. Almost no one in the world was identified as a gerontologist. Now there are over 5,000 professional members of the Gerontological Society of America. When I was an undergraduate there were no courses in gerontology. Now there are thousands of courses offered by most major (and many minor) colleges and universities. When I was an undergraduate there was only one gerontological journal (the Journal of Gerontology) begun in 1945. Now there are over forty professional journals and several dozen books in gerontology published each year.

The reasons for this dramatic growth are well known: the dramatic increase in numbers of aged, the shift from family to public responsibility for the security and care of the elderly, the recognition of aging as a "social problem," and the growth of science in general. It is less well known that this explosive growth in knowledge has developed the need for new solutions to the old problem of comprehending and "keeping up" with a field of knowledge. The old indexes and library card catalogues have become increasingly inadequate for the job. On-line computer indexes and abstracts are one solution but make no evaluative selections nor organize sources logically as is done here. These annotated bibliographies are also more widely available than on-line computer indexes.

These bibliographies will obviously be useful for researchers who need to know what research has (or has not) been done in their field. The annotations contain enough information so that the researcher usually does not have to search out the original articles. In the past, the "review of literature" has often been haphazard and was rarely comprehensive, because of the large investment of time (and money) that would be required by a truly comprehensive review. Now, using these bibliographies, researchers can be more confident that they are not missing important previous research; they can be more confident that they are not duplicating past efforts and "reinventing the wheel." It may well become standard and expected practice for researchers to consult such bibliographies, even before they start their research.

Dr. Aday, in his introduction, states that this bibliography is intended "to present a systematic collection of resources deemed useful in providing a more vivid picture of elderly as victims and criminals." He has provided a "broadbased guide to various references both in gerontology, criminology, criminal justice, and other allied fields." It is clear that this volume will be useful to human service professionals, especially those in criminology and corrections; but it also will be useful to researchers, teachers, students, attorneys, and law students in this field. I would add that it will be useful to any intelligent person, old or young, who wishes to find out what is known about crime and the elderly.

This field represents one of the most important concerns of both elderly persons as well as of criminologists and gerontologists. Although literature on this subject is of relatively recent vintage, the fact that this bibliography contains 361 references most of which were published since 1970, indicates how complex and extensive the field has become. It is clear that one cannot hope to comprehend even one aspect of this field without some such guide as this bibliography.

The author of has done an outstanding job of covering all the relevant information and organizing it into easily accessible form. Not only are the references annotated and organized into 10 chapters, but there is an author index and a comprehensive subject index with many cross-references for the items in the bibliography. Thus, one can look for relevant material in this volume in several ways: (1) look up a given subject in the subject index; (2) look up a given author in the author index; or (3) turn to the section that covers the topic. There is also a useful set of resources in Part III listing crime prevention programs, state agencies on aging, state correction agencies and organizations to contact.

Dr. Ronald Aday is an unusually qualified expert in this area because he has done so much research and writing in this area himself. This bibliography documents the fact that he has produced five chapters and papers important to this field, including the definitive review of crime in old age titled "Old Criminals" published in my Handbook on the Aged in the United States (item #259). His annotations are also concise and clear so that one can easily understand the essence of the reference and whether the original is worth pursuing.

So it is with great pleasure that we add this bibliography to our series. We believe you will find this volume to be the most useful, comprehensive, and easily accessible reference work in its field. I will appreciate any comments you care to make to be sent to me.

Erdman B. Palmore
Center for the Study of Aging and Human Development
Box 3003, Duke University Medical Center
Durham, NC 27710

INTRODUCTION

Since mid-century, there has been a significant shift in the focus upon the problems associated with the aging process. Relevant to this interest has been the dramatic increase in the elderly population. In the past two decades alone, the 65-plus population grew by 54 percent. In 1984, there were an estimated 50.2 million Americans age 55 or older and 28 million who were at least age 65. With the tremendous increase in the elderly population expected to continue well into the next century, various concerns associated with the aging process have emerged.

For example, crime and the elderly is one such area that has become an issue of increasing importance. A catalyst for this interest has been the growing awareness concerning the victimization of the elderly. Such adversity includes crimes of violence in the street and in the home, maltreatment within institutional settings, fraud, and abuse by family and other informal care providers. A recent report by the House Subcommittee on Health And Long-Term Care estimates that nearly 4 percent of all elderly Americans are abused, neglected, or exploited each year. This problem is expected to become even more severe as much of the future increase in the elderly population will occur in the physically, mentally and financially vulnerable over-75 age group.

Another important concern for students of crime and aging is the more recent disclosure of how the elderly are being increasingly viewed as perpetrators of crime. It has been suggested that the older offender in the criminal justice system comprises a unique category possessing special criminal and personal characteristics. Some have long histories of crime and a sequential career of institutional confinement. Yet others committed offenses relatively late in life and entered the criminal justice system for the first time as an elderly person. Deviance associated with the aging process itself, apprehension, custody, adjustment to prison life, family relations, and rehabilitation are just a few of the issues currently generating marked interest.

Both elderly offenders and victims present complex challenges in terms of accurate data collection, theoretical explanations, intervention programs and social policy issues. The purpose of this annotated bibliography is to present a systematic collection of resources deemed useful in providing a more vivid picture of the elderly as victims and criminals. An attempt is made to provide a broadbased guide to various references both in gerontology, criminology, criminal justice, and other allied fields. It is hoped that the development of this bibliography will serve to identify and arrange more comprehensively specific sub-topics in this rapidly growing field. Hopefully, such a process will provide a more efficient and useful integration of the references found in such a wide variety of disciplines.

SCOPE

Traditionally, gerontology as an emerging discipline has been primarily concerned with such topics as nursing care, disengagement, adequate housing, intergenerational concerns, and other psycho-social forces of aging. On the other hand, criminologists have been specifically concerned with the perplexing question of rising crime rates, prison reform, and a multitude of problems associated with youthful offenders. However, more recently these two disciplines have joined forces in addressing an emerging issue relevant to both. The integration of gerontology and the criminal justice fields respectively into a common framework requires a broad, yet well defined approach.

The primary scope of this annotated bibliography includes sources published, for the most part, in the United States since 1970. Researchers and policy makers began to address many issues associated with the elderly as victims in the early 70's. During this initial period, practitioners in gerontology and geriatrics as well as various levels of the criminal justice system began to focus on elderly victimization as an important social problem. Programs to reduce elderly victimization were quickly introduced, in some cases, before the problems were adequately defined. Conclusions from the 70's, while inconsistent, indicate that older persons are actual victims of crime much less frequently as a whole than the general population. However, the data does suggest that older people are more vulnerable and have greater fear of crime than the population as a whole. In addressing these issues, the literature contains reviews, victim profiles, training guides, crime prevention programs, and a variety of theoretical, policy, and research articles. In the early 80's, domestic abuse and violence became the central concern of the elderly victimization issue. Efforts have been made to include in this annotated bibliography a broad range of sources from this new and developing area.

The scope of the literature is more limited where the older offender is concerned. While a few articles and books periodically appeared throughout the 70's, the majority of research on older offenders has occurred in the past five years. The issue of elderly offenders has never achieved the same magnitude when compared to the victimization of the elderly. However, this does not imply that there is a lack of interest in this substantive area. For example, the Society for the Interdisciplinary Research on Elderly Offenders (SIREO) was formed in the early 80's to promote discussion and research on the topic of the elderly offender. In addition, four National Conferences on elderly offenders have been held to address various elderly offender issues. Many of the sources in this annotated bibliography come from a survey of the works contributed by SIREO members. Criminologists have been the most active in pursuing this interdisciplinary topic of study. This is reflected in the number of journal publications with a criminology or criminal justice emphasis. Few articles have really addressed the central problems of aging per se and the degree to which aging itself contributes to elderly crime and deviance.

Whether the issue is crime committed by the elderly or the elderly being victimized, an effort has been made to include a broad range of resources. Relevant research and policy articles from journals in gerontology, criminology, criminal justice, social work, sociology, psychology, law, and counseling have been included.

ARRANGEMENT

This topical bibliography includes 361 entries representing the most relevant literature on the subject of Crime and the Elderly. The book is organized into three separate parts. Parts I and II are arranged topically into five chapters each. Each of these chapters is arranged alphabetically by author. Part III includes several sections each of which is arranged alphabetically.

More specifically, Part I, "Crimes Against the Elderly," focuses on specific issues which appear to dominate the elderly victimization literature. Topics covered in Chapter 1, "Criminal Justice Issues," include those stressing the relationship of the elderly with the criminal justice system. Both theoretical and important policy issues pertaining to elderly attitudes toward and involvement with various components of the criminal justice system are included.

Chapter 2, "The Elderly as Victim," provides sources covering a broad range of topics. General victimization studies as well as specific types of crime committed against the elderly such as fraud, personal crimes, and crimes of violence are included. Numerous entries also involve surveys of those most vulnerable to crime. In particular, many of these entries involve data from surveys representing various parts of the country.

Chapter 3, "Fear of Crime," emphasizes those sources which are related to psychological and social factors, residential issues, and general demographic factors associated with elderly fear of crime. Several entries in this chapter also concentrate on national samples while others pinpoint fear of crime in specific geographic areas. Numerous "impact of fear" studies are also reviewed in this chapter.

Chapter 4, "Elder Abuse and Neglect," reviews topics centering on the family and medical environment as well as proposed causes and interventive strategies. Entries which stress assessment information and practitioner guides were sought out. Various policy related entries are also included.

Chapter 5, "Crime Prevention Programs," addresses topics related to protective services. Model programs which introduce victim assistance for the elderly and anti-crime programs and techniques are frequent entries. Finally, the elderly as an important resource in the fight against crime is an important theme in this chapter.

Part II, "The Elderly as Criminals," is also arranged into five separate chapters which address the major issues and concerns of this particular subject. Chapter 6, "Old Age and Crime," is similar in intent to the entries in Chapter 1, with the primary focus on aging offenders rather than victims. Important topics representing the entries in this chapter include the extent of elderly crime, age as a criminal defense, police and other criminal justice dilemmas and concerns as well as general social policy issues.

Chapter 7, "Elderly Crime Patterns," attempts to bring together those entries which serve to provide a profile of the aging criminal. Various topics such as property, sexual, alcohol and drug related offenses, and crimes of violence are identified. Entries in this chapter are characterized by both secondary data drawn from national samples as well as smaller, more homogeneous regional samples.

While somewhat limited, Chapter 8, "Causes of Criminal Behavior," includes several entries associated with the medical, social and psychiatric explanation of crime in old age. The majority of these entries focus on the correlates and causes of crime committed by the elderly. Included in this chapter are those sources which attempt to provde some insight into crime causation among those classified as chronic offenders when compared to those who commit crime for the first time late in their lives.

Chapter 9, "Aging Prisoners," introduces important entries centering on special problems of growing old in prison. Such topics as family relationships, passing time, long-term confinement, and the many consequences of imprisonment are reviewed. Numerous entries have important policy implications for the field of corrections.

Chapter 10, "Rehabilitative Programs," provides a collection of entries whose content scope includes special prison programs, including probation, and various community responses to the elderly offender. General issues relative to prisonization and problems of re-entry into the community are also commonly mentioned.

Part III, "Resources and Information," includes descriptions of ongoing crime prevention programs as well as correctional and aging agencies. Also, specific groups and organizations with a demonstrated interest in crime and the elderly are included.

Finally, the Author and Subject Indexes are keyed to the entry numbers in the Bibliography. The Author Index includes both authors and joint authors.

CONTENTS OF ENTRIES AND CITATION FORMAT

The annotated bibliography contains numerous types of references.

These include books, chapters from books, journal articles, conference proceedings, research reports, papers presented at professional meetings, Congressional hearings, unpublished manuscripts, dissertations, and special crime prevention models and training programs. Efforts are made to provide an assessment of the cited work, including objectives and major conclusions. Any unique contribution of the entry such as special information pertaining to social policy, elaborate tables, or a comprehensive reference section worthy of mention is also included. A consecutive numbering system is utilized beginning with "Chapter 1" and continuing through "Chapter 10." Every attempt was made to include a variety of sources that could be used both by practitioners as well as those engaged in traditional academic research.

ACKNOWLEDGEMENTS

Due to the dearth of published literature found in some of the special topics presented here, the compilation of this annotated bibliography has been a tedious endeavor. A special note of thanks goes to the various authors and organizations for the opportunity to include their material in this work. In particular, I would like to extend my appreciation to Evelyn Jared and Phila Chandler for their encouragement and many hours of assistance. Without them this project would never have become finished. The author also wishes to express his gratitude for the editorial assistance of Mary R. Sive and Loomis Mayer of Greenwood Press. Finally, thanks to Erdman B. Palmore, series editor, who invited me to prepare this annotated bibliography.

I CRIMES AGAINST THE ELDERLY

1 CRIMINAL JUSTICE ISSUES

001. Alston, L. (1986). <u>Crime and older Americans.</u> Springfield, Illinois: Charles C. Thomas, Publisher.

Drawing on numerous, diverse studies, the author synthesizes current knowledge of crime and older persons. The text is uniquely broad in scope, covering all types of crime and all sorts of institutions. It analyzes data on disreputable as well as vulnerable older persons, patterns of crime and the impact of such repercussions of crime involving older Americans. Community response to both older offenders and older victims is included. The author concludes with some predictions about crime and the elderly in the future and some suggestions about policy and practice. Appended to the text is a thorough bibliography.

002. Barnes, N. D. (1982). Crime and the elderly victim – a resource guide. <u>Council of Planning Librarians Bibliographies,</u> Chicago, IL.

A total of 115 entries compose this bibliography on the topic of crime effects upon elderly victims. The references cited concern the physical and mental effects of victimization upon the elderly, the fear of crime among the elderly, and the various attempts to deal with these problems. The bibliography includes monographs, journal and magazine articles, and government publications. All citations are listed in alphabetical order and are limited to those published between 1973 and 1981.

003. Boston, G. D. (1977). Crime against the elderly: a selected bibliography. <u>National Institute of Justice,</u> Rockville, MD.

This annotated bibliography focuses on literature in the area of elderly victimization and prevention. The bibliography consists of five topical areas: (1) victimization and the fear of crime, (2) prevention or deterrence, (3) defensible space and architectural design, (4) older citizen as volunteer court watcher, counselor, and volunteer law enforcement officer, and (5) crime prevention topics. The bibliography is arranged alphabetically by author within each section. The appendix contains a list of publisher names and addresses and a resource list of agencies and with a common interest in elderly victimization.

004.   Boston, G., Nitzberg, R. & Kravitz, M. (1979). Criminal
       justice and the elderly; a selected bibliography. National
       Institute of Justice, Rockville, MD.

Based on information published between 1971 and 1977, this annotated
bibliography includes materials found in the National Criminal Justice
Reference Service collection of elderly vulnerability to crime and the
role of elderly persons as active participants in the criminal justice
system. The entries are arranged alphabetically by author, title, or
journal source within seven separate sections. These include: general
nature of crimes against the elderly, crime impact on elderly lives
including fear and psychological damage, patterns and rates of
victimization, consumer fraud, victim assistance and financial aid,
community programs to curb elderly victimization, and changing image of
senior citizens due to their role in the criminal justice system.
Resource agencies and information on how to obtain cited documents is
provided.

005.   _____. Crimes and the elderly. (1978). Geriatrics,
33:93-94.

Examines the special problems of crime against the elderly. To combat
crimes against the elderly the Justice Department's Law Enforcement
Assistance Administration (LEAA), encouraged communities to adopt the
neighborhood watch program. This article further examines the statement
that "criminal activity has a much greater and lasting impact upon the
elderly, even though their crime victimization rate is lower than other
age groups."

006.   Cutler, N. E. (1977). Age and the future of American
       politics: from bicentennial to millenium 3. In Marlene A.
       Young Rifai (Ed.), Justice and Older Americans. Lexington,
       Massachusetts: D. C. Heath and Company.

This research takes a "macro" look into the future of the elderly
concerning political activity, attitudes, and expectations. It is
brought out that the people who will be old in the year 2000 are not the
same as those in the elderly category today. Society can expect the
elderly of tomorrow to be much more active in the political arena, as
well as organizational membership. Realizing the generational changes
that have taken place, the elderly of the future will be able to assert
a great deal of political influence. Four tables are included.

007.   _____. (1979). Elderly are least likely to become crime
       victims. Crime Control Digest, 13:8-9.

This study claims that the typical American victim of violent crime is
most likely to be poor, young, black, living with several roommates and
have a longer police record than the criminal involved. This profile of
a typical crime victim comes from the Justice Department's statistics
from the previous or past decade. In a disproportionate number of
cases, the article concluded from past research statistics, that
non-resistance is likely to keep the victim relatively safe from bodily
harm.

008. Goldsmith, J., and Goldsmith, S. S. (1976). Crime and
      the elderly: an overview. In Jack Goldsmith and Sharon S.
      Goldsmith (Eds.), Crime and the Elderly. Lexington,
      Massachusetts: D. C. Heath and Company.

In this essay, the authors call for the creation of a specialized index
of crimes against the elderly. Several reasons are given such as
vulnerability of the elderly, diminished resources, and environment and
social factors. Fear of crime is also discussed. Finally, the
emergence of victimology is discussed as it pertains to the elderly.
Criminal justice agencies are beginning to promote victim advocate
programs to assist the elderly through the system.

009. Goldsmith, J. (1976). Police and the older victim: keys
      to a changing perspective. Police Chief, 43(2), 18-20.

This article discusses the problem of crime and its relation to senior
citizens as being prime targets for victimization. Six keys were
devised to help understand the changing law enforcement on crime and
senior citizens. These keys relate to the changing nature of older
citizens society and to broad trends in contemporary policing. With the
aid of these six keys, movement is underway that is fostering a new look
and a redefinition of the older citizens in American society.

010. Goldstein, A. P., Hoyer, W. J. & Monti, P. J. (1979). Police
      and the elderly. Pergamon Press, Inc., Elmsford, NY.

This book written primarily for police officers presents basic
information concerning the reduction of crimes against the elderly and
stresses the reduction of the fear of crime. Physical and psychological
realities of aging are presented as being important factors for the
police to understand. Crime prevention is suggested as the best method
of reducing crime and the fear of crime among the elderly. Specific
training programs are suggested for helping senior citizens reduce their
fear of crime. Effective methods for working with the elderly through a
structured learning program is included. Tables and references are
provided in most of the chapters.

011. Gross, P. (1976). Law enforcement and the senior citizen.
      Police Chief, 43(2), 24-27.

Utilizes a survey constructed by the International Association of Chiefs
of Police, which was sent to the police departments in the nation's 500
largest cities and to a selected group of agencies including sheriff's
and county police departments. The purpose of the survey was to
identify current law enforcement activities that are staffed by senior
citizen volunteers and crime prevention programs aimed at the senior
citizen community. In developing special programs for senior citizens,
this article stresses that it is imperative that careful planning
precede program implementation. Senior citizens have participated in
and can successfully participate in the development and preparation of
crime prevention programs, and they are more than capable of providing
to the police agency voluntary services that would otherwise be
unavailable.

012.   Hofrichter, R. (1980). Neighborhood justice and the elderly –
        policy issues. National Council of Senior Citizens Criminal
        Justice and the Elderly Program, Washington, D. C.

This document (158 pages) is an exploratory policy study developed to
identify and consider selected issues in the design and practice of
neighborhood justice centers which may have important implications for
the elderly population. The present study involved an extensive
literature review as well as on site visits and interviews at selected
neighborhood justice centers serving a clientele which is more than 10
percent elderly. The centers provided the service of handling most
major types of disputes, and offering techniques for contacting senior
citizens. Brochures, program outlines, and a list of project sites are
included.

013.   _____. (1982). Impact of crime much heavier on the elderly.
        Crime Control Digest, 16:6-7.

This study, based on data from a National Crime Survey, found that
actual crimes against the elderly are extremely low, but the trauma and
economic impact of crime may affect older people more severely than
other population groups. When the elderly come within direct contact
with the offender, the elderly individual may become very frightened
even though it results in no injury. By altering their lifestyles to
minimize a special vulnerability to crimes of theft, the elderly are
forced to accept unwarranted limits on their freedom because of the fear
of violence.

014.   _____. (1983). Judicial access and the elderly: hearing
        before the Committee on Labor and Human Resources, United
        States Senate, July 12. United States Senate Committee on
        Labor and Human Resources, Washington, D. C.

The purpose of this testimony is to examine current federal, regional
and local efforts to provide legal services for the elderly. The
testimony focuses on how the special legal needs of the elderly are
being met by the Administration on Aging and by efforts of the private
bar. The document discusses the legal needs of the elderly and how they
are being met under Title III-B of the Older Americans Act. Included is
a summary of the accomplishments, new programs, and recently developed
strategies to better serve the legal needs of the elderly. Testimony by
representatives of agencies for the aging specifies particular needs and
further suggests ways in which such services might be expanded. This
report is 141 pages in length.

015.   Kerschner, P. A. (1977). Law, justice, and public policy.
        In Marlene A. Young Rifai (Ed.), Justice and Older Americans.
        Lexington, Massachusetts: D. C. Heath and Company.

The opening pages of this article carries a debate concerning the
generic approach versus the categorical approach in relation to
legislating public policy. The elderly have been trapped in a chaotic
system that attempts to use both. The author advocates continuing the
categorical approach, in essence targeting programs for the elderly. In
conclusion, the author uses the examples of health care, housing, and
income maintenance to illustrate how categorical programs have failed

due to an incorrect data base concerning the elderly. The crime problem
is also mentioned in the closing remarks.

016.   Levine, M. (1980). Research in law and aging. The
       Gerontologist, 20, 163-167.

The number of new publications concerning law and aging signals a need
for such work as the ever-growing elderly population increases. The
significance of the elderly has finally been realized. Many forms of
legislation affect the elderly, such as conservatorships, guardianships,
wills, taxes, etc., and over 60 federal laws concerning income,
employment, health care, housing, consumer affairs, and social service.
Most legal questions pertaining to the elderly involve interpretation
and administration of the statutes. Because old age is an ascribed
status, it will continue to be significant legally. Excellent article.
References.

017.   Liang, J., & Sengstock M. C. (1979). Aged victim's decision
       to invoke the criminal justice process. American Association
       of Retired Persons, Washington, D. C.

This study suggests that research on criminal victimization of the
elderly has focused on patterns of crime, consequences of victimization
and fear of crime, neglecting the victim's interaction with the criminal
justice system. Several research projects on crime reporting are
reviewed, with particular attention to the seriousness of crime as a
predictor of reporting. This study analyzed data collected through the
1973-1976 National Crime Survey conducted by the Census Bureau for LEAA
on persons over 60 who were victimized once by rape, robbery, assault,
burglary, larceny, or car theft. The seriousness of the victimization
was measured by the Sellin-Wolfgang scale. The study found that
seriousness of the crime was positively related to the likelihood of
reporting, although the victim's sex and the size of the community were
also factors. These findings offer some support to the notion that
nonreporting among the elderly can be attributed to the minor nature of
criminal incidents. Statistical tables and references are provided.

018.   Magann, A. (1975). Criminals no respecters of age.
       Perspective on Aging, 4(4), 17-22.

The focus of this article involves a description of a National
Conference on Crime Against the Elderly held June 5-7, in Washington, D.
C. Approximately 200 diverse participants from 25 states met to discuss
policy issues related to the elderly in the criminal justice system.
Speakers for the conference emphasized prevention, compensation for
victims, further awareness of crimes against the elderly, harsher
penalties, further research, and more respect for the elderly.

019.   Nathanson, P. A. (1977). Legal services. In Marlene A.
       Young Rifai (Ed.), Justice and Older Americans. Lexington,
       Massachusetts: D. C. Heath and Company.

This article basically describes the current activities of legal service
programs. In addition, the role and duties of the National Senior
Citizens Law Center (NSCLC) are described. Current areas of involvement
are involuntary commitment, guardianship, nursing home problems,

Medicare, Medicaid, pensions, Social Security, food stamps, and housing problems. Case studies are briefly sketched.

020.   Pope, C. E. & Feyerheim, W. (1976). The effects of crime on the elderly: a review of recent trends. Police Chief, 43(2), 29-32.

Examines the relationship between crime and the elderly. Utilizing several national studies, this article examines information taken from existing data sources including opinion polls and victimization surveys focusing on crime against the elderly. The purpose of the study was to determine the public's attitude toward aging and its perceptions from a senior citizens vantage point. In fact, fear of crime was reported as the major social problem affecting senior citizens.

021.   Renshaw, B. H. (1981). Crime and the elderly. Bureau of Justice Statistics Bulletin, U. S. Department of Justice.

Using data from the National Crime Survey, the Bureau of Justice Statistics examines crime against the elderly in several ways. An excellent review of elderly victimization is presented. Explanations for elderly victimization as well as the recent decrease in crime against the elderly are included. The report highlights the relative incidence of lesser and more serious crimes against the elderly. Several charts illustrate victimization rates for the years 1973-80.

022.   Rifai, M. A. Y. (1976). Older adult and the criminal justice system. Applied Systems Research and Development, Inc, Wilsonville, OR.

This research reports the results of a study completed in Portland, Oregon, on older Americans' attitudes about the United States criminal justice system. The study's data came from interviews with a random sample of 500 persons over age 60 in Portland. Additional information was collected from reviews of 300 police records of victims over age 60 and 50 in-depth studies of victims. A supplementary study was also conducted of selections from black neighborhoods. The findings indicate dissatisfaction of the elderly with the courts but strong support of police. Many elderly, in general, felt intimidated and confused by the criminal justice system. The elderly recommended establishing victims' counselors and restitution by criminals. Tables and references are provided.

023.   Rifai, M. A. (1977). Perspectives on justice and older Americans. In Marlene A. Young Rifai (Ed.), Justice and Older Americans. Lexington, Massachusetts: D. C. Heath and Company.

This is an introductory essay authored by the editor in which the themes and content of the book are presented. In sum, inequalities affecting the elderly are a result of a lack of social opportunities and a lack of societal protections. The economic, physical, and psychological inequalities make the elderly susceptible to crime. A society is considered unjust until it can protect both the rights of the offender and the victim.

024.   Schack, S., Grissom, G., & Wax, S. B. (1980). Police service

delivery to the elderly. University City Science Center,
Washington, D. C.

This study presents an overview of current knowledge and opinion about
the elderly's need for police service. A survey of 913 elderly
residents in two American cities is included. Despite the physical,
financial, and emotional suffering caused by victimization and fear of
crime, the elderly expressed extremely favorable attitudes toward the
police. The study also presents findings from a survey of 893 police
officers in the two cities to determine their attitudes toward the
elderly. The major problem for police is the difficulty in referring
elderly persons to appropriate sources for noncrime-related problems.
Police policy implications are included.

025. Schafer, C. H. (1980). Summary of 1980 legislation concerning
      crime victims and non-criminal matters with particular emphasis
      on older persons. National Retired Teachers Association,
      Washington, D. C.

This forty-six page document provides a summary of legislation proposed
or enacted during 1979-1980 that affects elderly persons in each state.
Data was collected from governor's offices. The summary provides a
brief description of bills and their status, as well as noting what
states did not consider legislation having special relevance for the
elderly. Various topics are included such as marketing of generic
drugs, the funeral industry, nursing homes, guardianship proceedings,
and death with dignity statutes. Florida, New Jersey, and Wisconsin are
among the states that have the most legislative activity that affect the
elderly.

026. Schmall, V. L., Ames, S. A., Weaver, D. A., and Holcomb, C. A.
      (1977).The legal profession and the older person: a shared
      responsibility. In Marlene A. Young Rifai (Ed.), Justice and
      Older Americans. Lexington, Massachusetts: D. C. Heath and
      Company.

It is stated at the outset that the legal profession has a tremendous
potential for helping the elderly. But, this potential is not being
realized. This article focuses on the perspective of both the elderly
and the legal profession. Arguments are raised as to why the elderly do
not take advantage of legal services. Likewise, the lawyer's
perspective explains why some attorneys are not so eager to represent
elderly clients. In conclusion, a method of sensitization has been
developed to aid professionals in dealing with the elderly. This
simulation exercise helps legal professionals confront the problems of
old age headon.

027. Sengstock, M. C., & Liang, J. (1979). Attitudes of the elderly
      toward the American legal system. American Association of
      Retired Persons, Washington, D. C.

This research provides a review of research on victims' treatment by the
courts. Data collected from the National Opinion Research Surveys
conducted between 1972 and 1977 are analyzed concerning the attitudes of
the elderly toward the justice system. An analysis of victim's
responses to their court experiences found that most were relatively

satisfied and discovered no significant differences between the elderly
and other age groups. However, victim advocacy programs could help
elderly individuals during the judicial process, but are opposed by many
judges and prosecutors. Tables and references are provided.

028.   Sicker, M. (1977). The elderly and the criminal justice
       system. Police Chief, 44(2), 38-41.

This article looks at the elderly as a target group of exceptional
concern that has recently begun to occur in the field of criminal
justice. The elderly themselves along with their supporters were late
to realize that they constitute a group particularly vulnerable to
criminal activity. The problems facing senior citizens are not enduring
nor are they contrived, they are problems that may be ignored by society
only at great risk to itself. The primary concern from a public policy
perspective should be on reducing the number of elderly victims, and on
limiting the vulnerability of the elderly.

029.   Sundeen, R. A. (1979). Differences in attitudes toward
       criminal justice agencies and practices: a comparative study
       among elderly. Justice System Journal, 5(1), 97-106.

Elderly persons from four communities in California were interviewed to
test the hypothesis that low-income elderly living in areas perceived as
criminally dangerous would be less supportive of police and more
punitive toward offenders than would more affluent elderly living in
areas perceived to be less threatening. Respondents were selected from
a planned retirement community and 3 senior citizen centers (n = 134).
Attitudes were measured by asking the respondents to rate the level of
effectiveness of four specific agencies, to state the purposee of
prisons, and to provide their preferred length of sentence for six
criminal offenses. It appears that indirect victimization can affect
attitudes and perceptions about criminal justice institutions.
Implications for social policy are suggested.

030.   Sunderland, G. (1979). Crime against the elderly in the
       United States - a practitioner's overview and response.
       National Retired Teachers Association, Washington, D. C.

This study focuses on the nature of crimes against the elderly and the
problems of the criminal justice system in responding to those crimes.
The need for local ongoing crime analyses to deal with specific local
crime problems is presented. While more data is available to analyze
crimes aimed at the elderly, the true causes of crime are unknown.
Suggestions with relevant policy implications are provided which focus
on crime prevention techniques, apprehension, and victim compensation.
An elaborate set of references is included in this 73 page document.

031.   Sykes, R. E. (1976). The urban police function in
       regard to the elderly: a special case of police community
       relations. In Jack Goldsmith and Sharon S. Goldsmith (Eds.),
       Crime and the Elderly. Lexington, Massachusetts: D. C.
       Heath and Company.

Described here is a study focusing on contacts between the elderly and
the police. Assessed is whether the elderly are at a greater risk and

the nature of consumption of police services by the elderly.   Three
questions asked were: (1) are police contacts with elderly more
frequent?; (2) what are the nature of police contacts?; (3) are police
contacts with elderly different than nonelderly? Observers rode with
the police in two cities with a combined population of 750,000. A total
of 4,918 encounters were recorded and studied. A very enlightening
discussion and conclusion section concludes the article.

032.   ____. (1985).   Topical bibliography: crime and the elderly.
        National Institute of Justice: Rockville, MD.

Based on information published since the early 1970's, this topical
bibliography includes 190 document abstracts representing the most
relevant literature on the subject of Crime and The Elderly in the
National Institute of Justice/NCJRS Collection. Specific topics covered
in this bibliography include crime prevention, fear of crime, victim
assistance, fraud, the relationship of the criminal justice system with
the elderly, and the elderly as criminals and prison inmates. In
addition, the bibliography also inludes victimization surveys and other
research orientated documents along with descriptions of criminal
justice programs designed to assist the elderly.

033.   Wetle, T., and Whitelaw, N.   (1977).   Person-centered
        service delivery. In Marlene A. Young Rifai (Ed.), Justice and
        Older Americans. Lexington, Massachusetts: D. C. Heath and
        Company.

The main goal of this article is to demonstrate how an elderly
individual might tie his/her personal supports into the formal social
services process. This is achieved by what is called the
"person-centered approach." Individual autonomy, acceptance, and
security for older persons is stressed. In addition, a critique of
current service delivery is provided. Among the major problems cited
are the duplication, rigidity, and lack of variety of many programs.
This article is theoretically based on the "systems" approach.

2 ELDERLY AS VICTIMS

034. Antunes, G. (1978). After-effects of crimes against elderly
      said intense. Crime Control Digest, 9, 2-3.

This article examines the belief that the after effects of crimes
committed against elderly persons may be worse than the crimes
themselves. Police, he feels, should treat such crimes as special cases
because "the aged are so tremendously vulnerable." In this article, the
author further states that elderly crime victims often isolate
themselves, become depressed and sometimes refuse to go out for fear of
becoming a crime victim again. This self-imposed exile to the home and
community environment may lead to problems ranging from depression to
death.

035. Antunes, G. (1977). Patterns of personal crime against the
      elderly: findings from a national survey. The Gerontologist,
      17(4), 321-327.

Based on personal interviews with a sample of approximately 375
respondents, this source stresses the societal concerns American
citizens have about the criminal victimization and fear of crime among
the elderly. Comparative rates of victimization are provided between
types of crime and elderly victims. Factors such as availability,
vulnerability and desirability are related to the victimization of the
elderly. Tables and references are provided.

036. Block, M. K., and Long, G. J., (1973). Subjective probability
      of victimization and crime levels: an econometric approach.
      Criminology, 24(2) 87-93.

In this 1965 N.O.R.C. study a subsample of 763 responses were analyzed,
in which the study found that there appears to be a significant positive
relationship between crime levels and subjective evaluations of
potential victimization. The study also found that there appears to be
no systematic relationship between specific victimization and specific
subjective probability. In the case of robbery, previous victims of
this offense have higher subjective evaluations than do non-robbery
victims; however, for burglary and burglary victims, the relationship is
reversed. Statistical tables are provided.

037. Butler, R. N. (1975). Victimization of the elderly. In <u>Why
      Survive Being Old In America.</u> New York: Harper & Row.

A most comprehensive overview of the elderly victimization is provided.
The causes, incidence, and effects of crimes committed against the
elderly are examined and suggestions for decreasing the frequency of
victimization are outlined. Particular emphasis is given to crimes of
violence as well as fraud and other basic forms of victimization.
Provides an important basis for policy implications including a greater
awareness of elderly victimization and its impact on the elderly
population.

038. Conklin, J. E. (1976). Robbery, the elderly, and fear: an
      urban problem in search of solution. In Jack Goldsmith and
      Sharon S. Goldsmith (Eds.), <u>Crime and the Elderly.</u> Lexington,
      Massachusetts: D. C. Heath and Company.

Examined in this article is the crime of robbery among the elderly,
their reaction to crime in general, and suggestions for minimizing the
risk of robbery. The elderly are said to be more vulnerable because of
decreased physical strength, include a disproportionate amount of women,
and no spouse (deceased) or children living with them. Utilizing data
gathered in Boston by the Center for Criminal Justice, 754 cases were
examined for this study. A discussion of fear of crime concludes the
article. Three tables, conclusions, and references are included.

039. Cook, F. L. & Cook, T. (1976). <u>Social Service Review,</u> 50(4)
      632-646.

Utilizing survey data this article examines the view that elderly
individuals have an exaggerated fear of crime. The level of fear the
elderly expresses is a function of demographic, ecological, physical,
and economic factors. There are four definitions that explain what
constitutes a crisis of victimization. These are: (1) relative fear of
being victimized, (2) relative severity of consequences of being
victimized, (3) increase in the rate of victimization, and (4) the
relative frequency of victimization. Tables and references are included.

040. Cook, F., Skogan, W., Cook, T., & Autunes, G. E. (1978).
      Criminal victimization of the elderly: the physical and
      economic consequences. <u>The Gerontologist,</u> 18(4), 338-349.

A comprehensive study that focuses on the physical, economic, and
environmental factors associated with aging that increases vulnerability
to criminal attack, and magnifies the impact of victimization. While
findings on financial losses show that the elderly are less likely than
others to be involved in crime, this congressional report concluded that
the elderly suffer disporportionately in qualitative measure from crime
victimization. Explanations for the high rates of fear among the
elderly are also addressed. Policy suggestions include compensation for
lost property for the elderly or for all persons suffering from physical
or property crimes. Tables are included which illustrate the survey
data and a bibliography is provided.

041. Cook, F., Skogan, W., Cook, T., & Autunes, G. E. (1975).

Crimes against elderly cited in senate welfare hearings.
Crime Control Digest, 9, 8-9.

These senate hearings discussed the question of why millions of elderly
Americans now live under a form of house arrest because of their
vulnerability to criminals. The author states that the nation is well
into a crisis situation regarding the criminal victimization of the
elderly. Because of their low incomes, the elderly are forced to live
in high-crime urban neighborhoods. This research supports strongly the
initial assumption that, of all persons who become targets of a criminal
act, the elderly usually suffer the most.

042.   Cook, F., Skogan, W., Cook, T., & Autunes, G. E. (19775).
       Crimes against elderly study set by Multnomah County Sheriff.
       Crime Control Digest, 9, 3-4.

Multnomah County, Oregon, is the site of one of the first empirical
social science studies to ever be conducted by an American police
department to research crime against older persons. Results of the
study were utilized nation-wide for development of specially tailored
crime prevention public education programs designed to reduce the
incidence of victimization of older Americans. The Multnomah County
study was proposed to help fill the significant lack of knowledge about
the problem. This study formed the basis for important policy decisions
and pointed out the need for additional research.

043.   Cunningham, C. L. (1976). Pattern and effect of crime
       against the aging: the Kansas City study. In Jack Goldsmith
       and Sharon S. Goldsmith (Eds.), Crime and the Elderly.
       Lexington, Massachusetts: D. C. Heath and Company.

This article is the result of a research project conducted by the
Midwest Research Institute on the metro Kansas City, Missouri area. Of
6,000 serious crimes reported against persons age 60 and over, 1800 of
these crimes were studied in detail. Interviews with victims, next of
kin, witnesses, and experienced ex-felons were also used. Among the
crimes studied were residential burglary, armed and strong arm robbery,
and larceny. Crime is defined in terms of social and economic
deprivations. Two tables, eight figures, conclusions, and implications
are included.

044.   Deluty, B. M. & Quay, H. C. (1984). Psychological impact of
       criminal victimization on the elderly. Academic Psychology
       Bulletin, 6(3), 271-285.

The authors examined whether an alternative classification system to the
traditional Uniform Crime Report (URC) would relate to the psychological
impact of crime on a sample of 100 victims ranging in age from 60-87.
Six descriptions of crime were developed to better describe the
respondents own experience and emphasize distinction between personal
and property crimes. Being the victim of a robber had a greater impact
than vandalism or burglary. Statistical correlations and 49 references
are provided.

045.   Dowd, J. J., Sission, R. P., & Dern, D. M. (1981).
       Socialization to violence among the aged. Journal of

Gerontology, 36(3), 350-61.

This research examined the attitudinal consequences of fear and victimization by focusing on the degree to which people of different ages express approval of violent behavior. The authors hypothesized that the experience of victimization socializes the individual to a view of violence, constituting an effective strategy for resolving interpersonal conflict. Data from a national sample supported this argument. Older people were less likely to be victims of crime, were more likely to report fear of crime, and were more disapproving of violent behavior than were younger people. Comprehensive statistical analysis is provided.

046. Dussich, J. P., & Eichman, C.J.   (1976). The elderly victim:
      vulnerability to the criminal act. In Jack Goldsmith, and
      Sharon S. Goldsmith (Eds.), Crime and the Elderly. Lexington,
      Massachusetts: D. C. Heath and Company.

Defined in this article is the concept of the "elderly victim syndrome." A lack of awareness exists concerning this problem because the mass media refuses to portray elderly victimization in their programming. An excellent literature review follows addressing whether the elderly are disproportionately victimized as compared to other groups. Vulnerability is then defined and several theoretical perspectives are critiqued (i.e., personal visibility paradigm). Two specific studies of Washington D. C. and Philadelphia conclude the article. References.

047. Edelhertz, H. (1978). Consumerism and the aging — the elderly
      as victims of fraud. Battele Human Affairs Research Center,
      Seattle, Washington.

This extensive report addresses the scope, character, and incidence of frauds and consumer abuse committed against the elderly, along with other significant factors believed to make the aged particularly susceptible to fradulent market operations. The research attempts to identify the range and distribution of fraud by classifying and describing the scope, and identifying the conditions under which the elderly are most susceptible to fraud. Other objectives of this project included an effort to develop guidelines and policy to make fraud less prevalent among aging populations; establish a body of information on how governmental and private organizations provide preventive actions; and establish a body of information on methods which can be used by public and private agencies to alert and educate the elderly to the dangers of fraud. Significant policy information is included.

048. Ehrlich, S. F. (1980). Somerset County, New Jersey: a
      victimization survey of the elderly. Somerset County College,
      Somerville, NJ.

A victimization survey of elderly residents of Somerset County was conducted to uncover relationships between crime victims and socioeconomic characteristics. Several variables were examined: age, amount of loss, education, family income, location of offense, marital status, number of household members, the victim's relation to household head, occupation, and value of dwelling or rental amount. A questionnaire was administered to a proportional sample of elderly households. Of the 417 senior citizens interviewed, 96 reported being victimized, with the 138 crimes varying from assault to petty larceny. The majority of the crimes concerned property rather than personal and over 83 percent of all crimes occurred within or near the home. Approximately 50 percent of all crimes were not reported to the police. Policy implications are suggested. The survey questionnaire, crime incident report and various tables are presented.

049.   Etzler, F. L. (1977). Crime and the senior citizen. Police
       Chief, 44(2), 58-59.

This article examines the effects of criminal victimization upon our elderly members of society. Many times, the gain to the criminal does not begin to compensate for the loss to the victim. Also, examined is the need for effective communication to reduce the victimization of elderly citizens and to establish an elderly citizen crime watch organization. The purpose of which, is not only to encourage the committed action of senior citizens by enabling them to run their own organization, but also free the police so they may communicate with other groups.

050.   Evans, K. & Leeds, M. (1976). Residential crime: the older
       person as victim. Police Chief, 43(2), 46-47.

This article explores several projects involving residential security and crime prevention for senior citizens. Special housing projects in Philadelphia, Pittsburg, and the state of Florida are described. It was found that older residents tended to be victimized by younger residents until architectural design changes especially for the elderly were implemented. Architecture was also used to define neighborhoods, a territoriality approach that fostered community acceptance of responsibility for crime prevention.

051.   Feinberg, N. (1978). Emotional and behavioral consequences
       of violent crime on elderly victims. Unpublished Dissertation,
       University of Pittsburg, Pittsburg, PA.

Provides a descriptive investigation of 50 elderly victims of robbery, burglary, or sexual assault who received help from the Alleghney County Center for victims of Violent Crime. Data were gathered from the agency's case records, interaction, observation and structured interviews. Distinguishing crime vulnerability characteristics of these victims as well as their informal and formal support systems were a major focus in this study. Important policy recommendations are included and implications for future research is suggested. Approximately 200 references are included.

052.   Fontana, A. (1978). Ripping off the elderly: inside the
       nursing home. In J. M. Johnson & J. D. Douglas (Eds.). Crime
       at the Top: Deviance in Business and the Professions.
       Philadelphia, PA: J. D. Lippincott.

Based on reported findings uncovered during field work by a researcher serving as a janitor in a nursing home in Southern California, this chapter outlines the vulnerability of the elderly in nursing homes and the impact of the total institution on the lives of those confined to

this particular facility. Observations included financial
misappropriations, drug abuse to control patients, isolation, violent
misbehavior, and neglect. Any patient not conforming to the prescribed
routine of the institution was considered a deviant and was treated as
such by both staff and other patients.

053. Fontana, A. (1980). Frauds against the elderly - health
      quackery - hearing before the house of representatives select
      committee on aging, October 1, 1980. US. Congress House Select
      Committee on Aging, Washington, DC.

This report focuses on frauds against the elderly in the area of health
quackery. Current law enforcement and regulatory efforts aimed at
dealing with such fraud are examined. Testimony before the House Select
Committee on Aging shows the extent to which the physical and financial
ills of the elderly make them vulnerable to fraudulent claims related to
health remedies and promises of increased income and investment
opportunities. Representatives from various regulatory agencies provide
testimony as to their efforts to combat advertisement and use of
fraudulent medical devices and drugs. Photographs and newspaper
clippings are included which illustrate various health frauds that have
been perpetrated.

054. Geis, G. (1976). Defrauding the elderly. In Jack
      Goldsmith and Sharon S. Goldsmith (Eds.), Crime and the
      Elderly. Lexington, Massachusetts: D. C. Heath and Company.

This article initially calls for the penalties of defrauding the elderly
to be increased. Briefly sketched is a historical review of how the
English courts have viewed fraud. The outlawing of lump-sum payments to
nursing homes is advocated. Excerpts from actual letters are presented
illustrating how some elderly victims are harassed by con-artists.
Finally, a stinging critique of how the courts denigrate the elderly
victim is included.

055. Geis, G. (1977). The terrible indignity: crimes against
      the elderly. In Marlene A. Young Rifai (Ed.), Justice and
      Older Americans. Lexington, Massachusetts: D. C. Heath and
      Company.

The elderly are called an "exploitable business commodity." The author
calls for the reformulation of the criminal codes to stiffen the
penalties of offenders convicted of crimes against the elderly. Also
discussed are elderly action groups which provide assistance to elderly
victims. Finally, factual illustrations are presented to show just how
susceptible to fraud the elderly are.

056. Goldsmith, J. and Thomas, N. (1978). Crimes against the
      elderly: a continuing national crisis. Aging, 281/282, (Mar-
      Apr.), pp. 23-25.

Examines the continuing national and urban crisis of crimes against the
elderly in terms of their physiological, economic, social, and
psychological vulnerability to criminal victimization. Actual and
perceived threat are two dimensions to the threat of criminal
victimization. Many neighborhoods and private groups, communities, and

states have introduced a number of experimental programs to protect the elderly.

057.   Groth, A. N. (1978). Older rape victim and her assailant. Journal of Geriatric Psychiatry, 11(2), 203-215.

Data relating to the rape of older women is presented based on data derived from clinical interviews and case records. Analysis of the information revealed that of the 170 offenders participating in the evaluation, 18 percent had been victimized women who were significantly older than the offenders. In addition, 12 percent of the offenders selected victims over the age of 50. The offenders were predominantly young, white, single males ranging in age from 12 to 38. The 42 victims ranged in age from 32 to 81. The majority of victims were sexually assaulted either in their own homes or in their own automobiles by complete strangers. The majority of offenders seriously injured their victims. It appears that age is no defense against rape and the older sexual victims are often targets of particularly brutal assaults.

058.   Gubrium, J. (1974). Victimization in old age: available evidence and three hypotheses. Crime and Delinquency, 20(3), 245-250.

Focuses on the operating principle and overwhelming belief, by the elderly that they as a group are prime targets of criminal victimization, and that they are subjected more so than any other group to criminal actions. This study utilizes a variety of surveys to measure the incidences of victimization and the variations in the rates of victimization. Three hypotheses are discussed to determine the impact of environmental protectiveness, and its relationship with increased criminal victimizations. Societal concerns about fear of crime, fear itself, age-concentration on victimization, and the possible effects of housing protectiveness are given a high amount attention.

059.   Hacker, G. A. (1977). Nursing homes: social victimization of the elderly. In Marlene A. Young Rifai (Ed.), Justice and Older Americans. Lexington, Massaachusetts: D. C. Heath and Company.

This article is highly critical of nursing homes. It is alleged that the social victimization of the elderly begins as one first enters a home. New residents often experience fear, confusion, depression, and loneliness. Several "horror stories" are illustrated, ranging from criminal incidents to incompetent staff employees. The final portion discusses the possible establishment of a nursing home ombudsman/paralegal system, to assist all patients with legal problems.

060.   Hahn, P. H. (1976). Crimes Against the Elderly: A Study in Victimology. Santa Cruz, CA.: Davis Publishing Company.

This book provides a general overview of the crisis situation involving crime against the elderly. Four major aspects of crime against the elderly are discussed. These topics include: (1) the fear of being criminally victimized, (2) the physical, emotional and financial effects of crime against the elderly, (3) the special vulnerability to criminal victimization of our elderly citizens, and (4) the high incidence of

crime of certain types, such as con games and consumer fraud, especially
in certain geographical regions and under certain circumstances. The
author suggests that the criminal justice system respond to the elderly
as a special category. Proposals for effectively dealing with crime
against the elderly are included.

061. Hochstedler, O. E. (1981). Crime against the elderly in 26
      cities. Albany, New York: Criminal Justice Research Center.

Available from the National Criminal Justice Reference Service, this 35
page report challenges many of the widely held beliefs about
victimization of the elderly. Based on data collected by the Bureau of
the Census, a most comprehensive profile of elderly victimization is
presented. Topics such as frequency, time and place, victim and
offender characteristics, victim-offender interaction are thoroughly
discussed. Numerous tables and charts are utilized to illustrate
elderly victimization data. The elderly (compared with younger age
groups) were: least likely to be injured, most likely to have their
purses snatched or their pockets picked, more likely to be victims of
completed vs. attempted crimes, and more likely to report offenses to
police.

062. Hofrichter, R. (1979). Victim compensation and the elderly:
      the programs in practice. United States Department of Justice
      Law Enforcement Assistance Administration. Ford Foundation,
      New York, NY.

This extensive report presents findings from a LEAA-funded study
focusing on victim compensation programs for the elderly. A total of 27
state programs were reported in operation to reimburse victims injured
in the commission of violent crimes. Problems which have surfaced in
the delivery of these services are outlined. General outreach
techniques such as the utilization of brochures, press releases, and
personal speaking engagements are discussed. Bureaucratic procedures
and police paperwork are blamed for the ineffective followup. The
document suggests that victim assistance services should include
referral networks with social service agencies and specific followup
procedures for abandoned cases. Included in the report is a list of
state victim compensation programs, names, addresses, and telephone
numbers of program directors, sample claim forms, sample legislative
bills factsheets, and other related information.

063. Jones, M. P. (1977). Victimization on Portland's skid row. In
      Marlene A. Young Rifai (Ed.), Justice and Older Americans.
      Lexington, Massachusetts: D. C. Heath and Company.

This article provides a graphic portrayal of what life is like on skid
row. Several case studies are presented dealing with elderly skid row
robbery and assault victims. These cases were obtained in part through
participant observation by the author. The "jackroller," or assailants,
are specifically defined into three categories. A study was conducted
by the Transit Bank of Portland, as a public service, to assess the
nature and extent of victimization. Final comments deal with the apathy
of witnesses, courts, and police to the skid row victim. Notes and
bibliography.

064.   Kahana, E., Liang, J., Felton, B., Fairchild, T., & Havel, Z.
        (1977). Perspectives of aged on victimization, ageism, and their
        problems in urban society. The Gerontologist, 17(2), 121-129.

In this study of 402 elderly persons, an initial attempt was made to
interpret the extent to which older persons living in two urban
communities are subjected to discrimination. The data shows that ageism
exists within a small minority of the elderly population.
Socio-economic status tends to determine the level and magnitude of
discrimination and victimization the elderly face. Community and
neighborhood problems, including fear of crime, appeared to be of
primary concern to older persons.

065.   _____   (1977). Kentucky hosts statewide discussion on crime
        and the elderly. Crime Control Digest, 11, 3-4.

Discussed is the problem of criminal victimization against senior
citizens by members of the State Department of Justice, the area
development districts and senior citizens groups at a conference in
Lexington, Kentucky. According to Jack Smith, Secretary of Justice, the
elderly in Kentucky are one of the most vulnerable groups when it comes
to crime, both economically and physically. Also, examined in this
article was a means of getting the state and local agencies that serve
the elderly together to share ideas and resources, in order to better
formulate a criminal justice plan to meet the needs of the elderly.
Discussion at the conference focused on ways to further educate the
elderly in crime prevention techniques.

066.   Kosberg, J. I.   (1985). Victimization of the elderly: causation
        and prevention. Victimology, 10(1), 376-396.

This article stresses that the elderly are especially vulnerable to
victimization due to their living arrangements, physical
characteristics, economic needs, and social losses, as well as to
societal attitudes and values. Included for discussion are the causes
of crime against the elderly in the home and on the street by strangers,
maltreatment of geriatric populations within institutional settings, and
elder abuse by family, friends, and neighbors. Efforts for the
prevention of the victimization of the elderly are described and are
related to their dependency, isolation, and powerlessness. The need for
cross-cultural research is stressed. Extensive references.

067.   Leeds, M. & Evans, K.   (1976). The older person as victim:
        residential crime. Police Chief, 43(2), 48-51.

Discusses in an indepth fashion the plight of the elderly, as being more
vulnerable to residential crime, than any other segment of our
population. Utilizing several studies and/or projects, programs aimed
at reducing crime against the elderly are being implemented to ease the
elderly persons fears of being victimized. Examined in this article are
several strategies presented to help the project residents exercise more
control over the crime in the area and ultimately over their own lives.
Also, examined in this article is the efforts to alert the elderly to
the importance of community organization, which must be accompanied by
awareness of their critical role in helping promote neighborhood
security.

068.   Liang, J., & Sengstock M. C.   (1981).   The risk of personal
       victimization among the aged.   Journal of Gerontology, 36(4),
       463-471.

This study examines the risk of personal victimization as a function of
the effects of individual characteristics and environmental conditions.
Victimization in this case includes such crimes as rape, robbery,
assault, and personal larceny.   Utilizing data from the National Crime
Survey, over 20,000 respondents over the age of 65 are included in the
study.   An elaborate statistical analysis is provided.   Based on the
fact that the authors develop a predictive model of victimization,
several important suggestions are made concerning future research.

069.   Malinchak, A. A. & Wright, D.   (1978).   Older americans and
       crime: the scope of elderly victimization.   Aging, 281-282
       (March/April), 10-16.

The extent to which criminal victimization of the elderly persists is
addressed.   Current confusion about the national problem of crimes
against the elderly is due to the fact that elderly victims often do not
report crimes, law enforcement officials are not aware of the special
needs of the elderly crime victims, and the subject of elderly crime
victimization has been approached in a bandwagon fashion.   The authors
raise pertinent questions concerning the validity and reliability of the
instruments used to collect victimization data.

070.   McClelland, K., Faletti, M. V., Quay, H. C., & Johnson, V. S.
       (1980).   Victim characteristics, crime type, and the immediate
       impact of crime on elderly victims.   Paper presented at the
       Annual Meeting of the Gerontological Society, San Diego,
       California.

Research findings is based on interviews with 160 elderly crime victims
in Dade County, Florida.   The major focus involved an examination of
relationships among the impacts of the crime on the victim, the types of
crime involved, and the victim's social and economic characteristics.
Victims were identified for an initial interview by trained police
officers 48 to 72 hours following the report of the crime.   A total of
160 elderly victims were interviewed and 95 of these gave followup
interviews 4 to 6 months later.   Impact of victimization was measured by
the debility scale based on effects on health, increased fearfulness,
and suspension and the isolation scale which involved increased
self-protective behaviors, purchase of equipment to improve physical
security, reduced mobility and independence in daily living activities,
and social withdrawal.   Due to the wide variance in impacts reported by
victims, the study cautioned future researchers about the complexities
involved in victimization surveys of the elderly.

071.   McGuire, M. V. & Edelhertz, H.   (1980).   Consumer abuse of
       older Americans: victimization and remedial action in two
       metropolitan areas.   In G. Geis, & E. Stotland, (Eds.),   White
       Collar Crime: Theory and Research.   Beverly Hills, CA: Sage
       Publications, Inc.

Research for this chapter is designed to explore the nature and extent

of consumer frauds and abuses against persons 55 years and older.
Consumer abuse was studied in Genesee County, Michigan and King County,
Washington. These two separate studies examined the complaints filed in
two local consumer protection offices by older consumers during a
6-month period. In addition, a community survey involved telephone
interviews with older residents of the communities. Findings indicated
that complaints filed by older consumers in local consumer protection
offices did not differ from those filed by younger consumers. The
research suggests that older victims of consumer fraud tend to
underreport their experiences of victimization. A significant
proportion of respondents who sought help, however, felt their consumer
abuses were not rectified. Statistical data and references are
provided.

072. Newman, E. S., Nelson, A., Van Buren, D. (1975). <u>Crimes
      against the elderly in public housing: policy alternatives.</u>
      State University of New York at Albany, Albany, NY.

This monograph is based on a survey of elderly residents in three types
of public housing environments. Discussion focuses on the implications
of age-segregated housing with respect to incidence of crime and fears
about crime among the elderly. The purpose of the study was to explore
the effects of these different living arrangements (age-integrated,
age-segregated, and age-segregated units within an age-integrated
project) on the numbers and kinds of crimes involving elderly victims.
Based on the findings, the authors favor a policy of encouraging
age-segregated public housing for the elderly.

073. Ragan, P. K. (1977). Crimes against the elderly: findings
      from interviews with blacks, mexican americans, and whites.   In
      Marlene A. Young Rifai (Ed.), <u>Justice and Older Americans.</u>
      Lexington, Massachusetts: D. C. Heath and Company.

This is a cross-ethnic study whose purpose is to dispel the following
stereotypes: (1) crime is a very serious problem facing most older
people, (2) crime affects the elderly more than other groups, (3) the
typical victim is an elderly white woman. Utilizing the data gathered,
each stereotype was dispelled. Findings from similar surveys are
presented as well. Finally, limitations, distortion, and
advantages/disadvantages of data are presented. Two tables.

074. Reiman, Jeffrey H. (1976). Aging as victimization: reflections
      on the American way of ending life. In Jack Goldsmith and
      Sharon S. Goldsmith (Eds.), <u>Crime and the Elderly.</u> Lexington,
      Massachusetts: D. C. Heath and Company.

This is an emotionally written essay about the status of the elderly in
our present society. Because the aged are viewed as less valuable,
people commit crimes against the elderly because they know that society
as a whole does not really care. Thus, aging itself has been rendered a
process of victimization. Our institutions and the media glorify youth.
We have chosen "legitimate" victims; i.e., blacks, women, elderly, etc.,
in which the elderly are not one of the "normal" folk. If one needs
help or assistance in America, that person is scorned by society.
Finally, the author states that we force the elderly to retire and into
nursing homes to die with people they do not even know.

075.   Richardson, J. B. (1976). Purse snatch: robbery's ugly
       stepchild. In J. Goldsmith and S. S. Goldsmith (Eds.),
       Crime and the Elderly. Lexington, Massachusetts: D. C. Heath
       and Company.

This article focuses attention on the seriousness of purse snatching and
the problems law enforcement agencies have in dealing with it. A
profile of the victim is illustrated as being an elderly female, poor,
living alone, victimized while in route to the store or waiting for
public transportation. They also have rigid lifestyle habits. A
profile of the suspect shows that juveniles overwhelmingly make up this
category. The Portland, Oregon Police Department Crime Analysis Unit is
mentioned, illustrating its functions and results. An itemized list of
what law enforcement agencies can do conclude the article. Three
tables.

076.   Rifai, M. A., & Ames, S. A. (1977). Social victimization
       of older people: a process of social exchange. In Marlene A.
       Young Rifai (Ed.), Justice and Older Americans. Lexington,
       Massachusetts: D. C. Heath and Company.

This chapter focuses on the relationship between the justice system and
the elderly. Utilizing the exchange model, the authors discuss how
social victimizatiion occurs when individuals are adversely affected by
certain aspects of society which he/she has little or no control. Laws
related to economics, consumer problems, age discrimination, protective
services, and nursing homes serve as evidence of the social
victimization of older people. The justice system's failure to meet the
needs of the elderly results from the fact that the laws themselves are
problematic and/or not enforced, and that older people lack legal
representation and easy access to the courts. Strategies for improving
legal services are discussed.

077.   Singer, S. I. (1974).   The elderly as victims of crime: a
       study of crime against the elderly in an urban environment.
       Unpublished Ph.D. dissertation. Boston, Massachusetts:
       Northeastern University.

This research reviews the types of crimes committed against the elderly,
the offender who commits them, why the elderly are selected as victims
and the consequences of their victimization. As a result of research
findings, the study concludes that the elderly's victimization may or
may not increase in comparison to other age groups because of various
factors. Based on these findings, a general hypothesis on
environmental, economic, physical, and psychological vulnerability is
suggested. Suggestions are more for reducing the elderly's
vulnerability and thus minimizing the effect of crime.

078.   Tighe, J. H. (1977). A survey of crimes against the elderly.
       Police Chief, 44(2), 30-31.

This article is a summary of major findings and conclusions from a
general police survey of the conditions and circumstances affecting
elderly victimizatiion in Miami Beach, Florida. A description is
provided for the elderly victim as well as those most likely to commit
crimes against them. Policy recommendations based on survey results
include increased public education and crime prevention information

efforts, such as printed materials, onsite security inspections, and a victim follow-up program.

079.   Viano, E. C. (1983). Victimology: an overview. In J. I. Kosberg (Ed.), Abuse and maltreatment of the elderly: causes and interventions. Littleton, Massachusetts: John Wright, PSG, Inc.

This chapter provides a comprehensive examination of the terminology and issues surrounding victomology. Historical developments which focuses on theoretical discussions of survival and individual responsibility are presented. New research perspectives on victimology are outlined and fully analyzed. Applications are made to the elderly population which are presented as significantly increasing and defined as increasingly vulnerable, dependent, and in need of protection. Excellent theoretical chapter with a comprehensive bibliography.

080.   Viano, E. C. (1976). Crimes, victims, and justice. In Jack Goldsmith and Sharon S. Goldsmith (Eds.), Crime and the Elderly. Lexington, Massachusetts: D. C. Heath and Company.

The opening paragraphs of this article illustrate the increased popularity of victimology as a discipline. A brief historical presentation of victim compensation is included. From the present victimology studies, three varieties of interest have emerged: (1) scientific – causal association of victim and offender, (2) social engineering – reducing hazards of victimization, increase chances of offender detection, and (3) legal and moral – accurate assignments of responsibility, blame, fault, guilt, etc. An itemized list of new perspectives provided by victim research are presented, as well as limitations and risks of victim centered research. References are provded.

081.   Yin, P. H. (1985). Victimization and the Aged. Springfield, IL.: Charles C. Thomas.

This text stresses concepts, typologies and theories of crime victimization of older people. The author presents in-depth coverage of robbery, burglary and theft, fear of crime, effects of victimization, fraud, elder abuse, and the criminal justice's treatment of older victims. While the approach to victimization in this work is rather narrow, the approach does emphasize the interface of criminology, victimology and gerontology. This comprehensive review of the research literature from these and other disciplines provides substantive correction to many widely held views on the subject. An extensive bibliographic reference section is evidenced by 256 entries. There is also both a subject and author index.

082.   Venters, K. & Thompson, R. D. (1978). Crime and the senior citizen: a victimization study of the elderly in Chattanooga, Tennessee. University of Tennessee at Chattanooga Criminal Justice Department, Chattanooga, TN.

Based on a large survey in the Chattanooga area, this research attempts to document the extent and impact of victimization found among the elderly population. Utilizing a total of 1,003 responses, 120 (12 percent) indicated that they had been victims of crime. Respondents were divided by age into two categories: 60 through 69 and over 70 years of age. Fear and feelings of insecurity seem to be more prevalent for those in the over 70 category. Suggestions for crime prevention are discussed and policy recommendations were made. Tables, the survey instrument and an extensive bibliography are included.

3   FEAR OF CRIME

083. ____ . (1978). Afraid to go out at night. <u>Crime Control</u>
      <u>Digest,</u> 12(2), 6-7.

Utilizing a study completed by the Montgomery County Department of
Police, it was determined that 85% of the elderly of Montgomery County,
Maryland, are afraid of being out of their homes, to the extent that
many won't go out at night or ride public transportation. The survey
also showed that out of 178 elderly residents in Silver Spring,
Maryland, 24 percent of those who were interviewed has been victims of
at least one actual or attempted crime in the past five years. The
survey is one of three parts of a federal grant given the MCDP's Crime
Prevention Unit who aim to reduce the public's fear and vulnerability to
crime through research of the crime problem, public education of
prevention techniques, and a victim assistance program.

084. Baldassare, M. (1986). The elderly and fear of crime.
     <u>Sociology and Social Research,</u> 70(3), 218-221.

This article briefly explores the causes of fear of crime among the
elderly. Such topics as social status, social interaction, and
well-being were examined as important intervening variables between age
and fear of crime. The sample utilized in this study consisted of 1,009
residents of Orange County, California. After interviewing this initial
sample via telephone, a sub-sample of 106 persons aged 65 and older were
identified. One variable, income, reduced to insignificance the
relationship between age and fear of crime. The low income elderly were
the most vulnerable to the fear of crime. It was concluded that old age
combines with low income to produce greater fear. Tables and references
are included.

085. Clemente, F. & Kleiman, M. (1976). Fear of crime among the
      aged. <u>The Gerontologist,</u> 16(3), 207-210.

Utilizing national survey data this research compares the patterns of
fear of crime among the aged and the non-aged. Sex, race, socioeconomic
status, and size of the community were the four major variables used in
the analysis. Findings suggest that the older population are not a
homogeneous group but some segments are more fearful than others. For

example, female, black, or metropolitan residents possess extremely high fear rates. Provides policy implications for practitioners seeking to control fear of crime among the aged.

086.   Clemente, F. & Kleiman, M.   (1977).   Fear of crime in the United States: a multivariate analysis. Social Forces, 56(2), 519-531.

This social survey included 2,700 aged individuals incorporated to obtain a multivariate perspective on the determinants of fear of criminal victimization. A most comprehensive profile of fear in the United States is presented. Special attention is given to the elderly as a group. Actual fear is presented as a greater problem than crime itself. A thorough statistical analysis and interpretation of findings is presented. Bibliograhy is most extensive in nature.

087.   Cutler, S. J.   (1980).   Safety on the streets: cohort changes in fear. International Journal of Aging and Human Development, 10(4), 373-384.

Utilizing data from a 1965 A.I.P.O. Gallup Poll and the 1976 N.O.R.C. general social survey, the responses of five birth cohorts were conducted to determine whether observed age changes in being afraid to walk alone at night are consistent with interpretations that stress characteristics of the aging process to account for the elderly's greater fear of vulnerability to criminal victimization over an eleven year period. Because all cohorts shared in the increasing fear for their safety, this suggested that the existence of a period effect in which generally heightened levels of fear have resulted from increasing crime rates. As a result the fear level impedes almost every facet of the elderly citizens life.

088.   Donnermeyer, J. F., Phillips, G. H., & Steiner, M. J.   (1983). Fear of crime and victimization in rural areas. Paper presented at the North Central Sociological Association annual meeting, Cleveland, Ohio.

This paper examines the proportion of elderly victimized by three major types of property crime (vandalism, burglary, and household larceny) and compares the extend of victimization between the younger and older respondents from the study. The authors also review characteristics of rural elderly victims and provides a comparative analysis of attitudes toward crime between the older and younger respondents. The paper further explores the impact of victimization to the rural elderly with respect to their perceived seriousness of crime and feelings of personal safety. Information for the paper is based on a rural victimization study conducted in Pike County, Indiana, using telephone interviews with 366 households. Older rural persons were less likely to always feel safe than younger rural persons, and rural older persons who had experienced at least one property crime victimization were far less likely to feel safe than rural older nonvictims. Tables and references are included.

089.   Dowd, J. J.   (1981).   Socialization to violence among the aged. Journal of Gerontology, 36(4), 350-361.

As part of a 1976 General Social Survey conducted by the National
Opinion Research Corporation, 1,499 interviews were taken to assess the
degree to which respondents of different ages express support for
violent behavior; and more specifically to investigate some of the
attitudinal consequences of fear and victimization. As a basis for
resolving interpersonal conflict, that the individual learns through
socialization that violent behavior is often associated with the
attainment of a certain goal. This research also addresses the fact
that older people are more likely to report the fear of crime more so
than the actual crime itself, even though they are less likely to be
victims of crime than younger persons.

090.   Eve, S. B. (1985). Criminal victimization and fear of crime
       among the noninstitutionalized elderly in the United States:
       a critique of the empirical research literature. Victimology,
       10(1), 397-408.

The empirical research literature on criminal victimization and fear of
crime among older adults is reviewed and critiqued. The literature
indicates that older adults are generally less likely to be victimized
than younger adults are but more likely to be fearful of being a crime
victim. According to the author, a critical assessment of the
literature suggests that these differences may be exaggerated by
methodological flaws including not controlling for risk factors.
Suggestions for improving the research methodology and theory of
victimization studies are discussed. It is also suggested that
cross-cultural comparative studies are needed to begin to identify
societal determinants of victimization. Specific ways in which this
research can be accomplished are suggested. References are included.

091.   Eve, R. A., & Eve, S. B. (1984). The effects of powerlessness,
       fear of social change, and social integration on fear of crime
       among the elderly. Victimology, 9(2), 290-295.

The article attempts to explain why many elderly are afraid of crime in
circumstances where their actual risk of criminal victimization tends to
be low. Data on a sample of 8,065 adults 60 years of age and older in
Texas were analyzed using multiple classification analysis techniques.
It was hypothesized that fear was often a symbolic fear which had its
origins in diffuse anxiety concerning the future in a rapidly changing
society where the elderly tend to be relatively powerless. It was found
that those elderly in the most powerless categories were the most
fearful of crime.

092.   _____. (1980). Fear of teenagers greatly affects life for the
       nation's elderly. Crime Control Digest, 14:9-10.

This study conducted by Pennsylvania State University utilized 2,000
elderly citizens to determine the level of fear and victimization by
teenagers. Approximately ninety percent of the elderly citizens
surveyed stated that they actually change their direction of travel or
cross the street just to avoid teenagers. This research brief concluded
that the fear of teenagers is so great elderly persons living in urban
areas often remain in doors becoming prisoners in their own homes. A
limited statistical analysis is provided.

093. Finley, G. E. (1983). Fear of crime in the elderly. In J. I.
      Kosberg (Ed.), Abuse and maltreatment of the elderly: causes
      and interventions. Littleton, Massachusetts: John Wright, PSG.

This chapter contributes a thorough overview on the fear of crime in the
elderly. Issues such as victimization risk and fear of crime, physical
and financial consequences, psychological and behavioral consequences
are addressed. Utilizing a comprehensive literature review, correlates
and causes of fear of crime are indexed. Programs and materials
reducing crime and fear of crime among the elderly are suggested.
Excellent policy chapter with an extensive bibliography.

094. Garfalo, J. (1979). Victimization and the fear of crime.
      Journal of Research in Crime and Delinquency, 16(1), 80–97.

A series of victimization surveys conducted in eight American cities
which helped stimulate policies and programs aimed at reducing the fear
of crime. Important variables discussed include: actual risk, role
socialization, perceived protection, the media, and the experience of
victimization. A profile of respondents most likely to experience the
fear is presented. In addition, a working model to reduce the fear of
crime is also presented. Tables and references are especially helpful.

095. Greenstein, M. (1977). Fear and nonreporting by elders: an
      invitation to law enforcement. Police Chief, 44(2), 46–47.

This study examines the link between fear of crime and the high rate of
nonreporting among the elderly, and advocates a system of support for
the victim as a way to increase confidence in law enforcement. The
major focus of the support system includes crime prevention education
and victim service components. While brief in content, this article
serves as an excellent source in addressing the issue of nonreporting.
Suggestions are made which have a direct bearing on policy for law
enforcement officials.

096. Gubrium, J. F. (1973). Apprehensions of coping incompetence
      and responses to fear in old age. International Journal of
      Aging and Human Development, 4(2), 111–125.

The variety of fear focused upon in this exploratory study was conceived
as stemming from perceived incompetence in coping with daily events.
Expressions of fear by elderly persons were examined and classified
according to special sources. The survey indicated that the aged
express fear of personally unpredictable and/or uncontrollable events
that are individual or lie in their social environment. Also, numerous
suggestions and strategies were devised for reducing fear in senior
citizens. Excellent source to develop theoretical basis for elderly
fear.

097. Hazel, Z. & Broderick, K. (1980). Victimization and fear of
      crime among the urban aged. Police Chief, 47(3), 34–36, 65.

Based on 1,617 respondents attending a Senior Safety and Security
Program, a typology of urban fear among the elderly is proposed. Fear
of crime is measured by various environmental locations (i.e., home,

neighborhood, car, public transportation and donation) rather than
perception and morality. The Cuyahoga County Commissioners' Safety and
Security Program is described as an attempt to counter victimization and
fear of crime among the aged. A limited statistical approach is
included, but the basis of the article is policy oriented and includes
some valuable suggestions.

098.   Janson, P. & Ryder, L. K. (1983). Crime and the elderly: the
        relationship between risk and fear. The Gerontologist, 23(2),
        207-212.

Utilizing data from a Los Angeles community survey of 1,269 people
between the ages of 45 and 74, this research investigated the
relationship between the elderly's concern with crime and the
neighborhood's crime rate. An interesting comparative analysis is
conducted between Anglos, Blacks and Mexican Americans and the variables
under study. Strategies for crime prevention are discussed.

099.   Jaycox, V. H. (1979). Elderly's fear of crime - rational or
        irrational? Victimology, 3(3-4), 329-334.

This study reports that victimization surveys have shown that elderly
persons are more fearful of personal crimes than are younger persons. A
neighborhood-based study in which telephone interviews were conducted
with 1600 elderly residents of 8 neighborhoods in 4 cities found a link
between fear of crime and actual victimization experience. The
respondents who were most afraid of crime were those who lived in the
most dangerous neighborhoods. Findings indicate that fear of crime
among elderly persons is not irrational but rather a response to
external and internal realities associated with advanced age. Tables
and references are included.

100.   Jeffords, C. R. (1983). The situational relationship between
        age and the fear of crime. International Journal of Aging
        Human Development, 17(2), 103-111.

Centering on a crime poll of 2987 respondents, this research focuses on
fear of crime and the relative danger of walking in the neighborhood as
opposed to the safety of one's home. Age was found to be significantly
related to the fear associated with the relative danger of walking in
the neighborhood. The need to establish more comfort in the immediate
neighborhood is discussed. General conclusions and future research
implications are somewhat useful. Helpful tabular information included.

101.   Lawton, M. P. & Yaffe, S. (1980). Victimization and fear of
        crime in elderly public housing tenants. Journal of
        Gerontology, 35(5), 768-779.

In an attempt to investigate victimization and fear of crime in public
housing, a study of 662 elderly tenants in 53 public housing sites was
conducted to measure the fears and crime related experiences of the
elderly. Both cross-sectional and longitudinal data are analyzed which
provide a more comprehensive answer to the research question. Of special
importance in this resarch is the attempt to develop a profile of
respondents residing in predominantely age-segregated living

environments. A thorough statistical analysis and interpretation of
results is presented. Relevant references related to fear within the
environment is noteworthy.

102. Lawton, M. P., Nahemow, L., Yaffe, S. & Feldman, S. (1976).
      Psychological aspects of crime and fear of crime. In J.
      Goldsmith and S. S. Goldsmith (Eds.), Crime and the Elderly.
      Lexington, Massachusetts: D. C. Heath and Company.

This article explores the relationship of three variables, actual
victimization, exposure to crime, and the fear of crime, on both the
psychological and social level of the elderly individual. Active
mastery and internal/external locus of control are discussed pertaining
to the psychological make-up of the elderly. The results of a follow-up
study conducted by the Philadelphia Geriatric Center and M.I.T. of 53
low-rent public housing environments nationwide are presented.
Conclusions, generalizations, and references follow.

103. Lebowitz, B. D. (1975). Age and fearfulness: personal and
      situational factors. Journal of Gerontology, 30(6), 696-700.

This article focuses on the relationship between age and reports of
fear. Secondary data is presented as a means of testing the personal and
structural factors associated with fear of walking around one's
neighborhood. While the direct effect of age on fear was minimal,
significant age differentials on fear were found by income, size of city
residence, and the presence or absence of others in the household.
Important suggestions for future research are provided along with tables
and references.

104. Lee, G. L. (1983). Social integration and fear of crime among
      older persons. Journal of Gerontology, 38(6), 745-750.

Focusing on a large sample of 2,832, this research tested the hypothesis
that fear of crime is inversely proportional to social integration among
elderly adults. The study provides an excellent and highly reliable
7-item scale designed to measure fear of crime. The most important
antecedents were measures of previous personal victimization and
victimization of acquaintances. While the dimension of social
integration plays only a minor role in the causal structure of fear of
crime, new directions for research are presented. Tabular data and
numerous references are appended.

105. Lee, G. R. (1982). Residential location and fear of crime
      among the elderly. Rural Sociology, 47(4), 655-669.

This research examines the hypothesis that fear of crime is greater
among the urban than the rural elderly. The sample utilized to test the
hypothesis consists of over 4,000 residents of Washington State aged 55
and over. A useful measure of individual anxiety about criminal
victimization was constructed by means of a factor analysis. Using this
measure, fear is greatest among farmers and urbanites. Several sex
differences in the relationship between residential location and fear of
crime are also observed. Implications for research, theory and policy
are discussed.

106. Leeds, M. & Evans, K. (1976). Residential crime: the older
      person as victim. The Police Chief, 43(2), 46-47.

This article focused on residential dwellings as a prime target for
victimization. Numerous residential neighborhoods are investigated.
Utilizing the survey method, collected information is used to reveal
levels of fear of crime and the behavioral changes arising from this
fear. Strategies are presented to aid elderly residents in exercising
control over the crime in their area. Policy implications for
neighborhood watch programs are suggested. Several references.

107. Lindquist, J. & Duke, J. (1982). The elderly victim at risk:
      explaining the fear victimization paradox. Criminology, 20(1),
      115-126.

The major focus of this research is to address the important issues
associated with the problem of victimization of the elderly. Based on a
comprehensive survey, the data suggest that the victimization problem of
elderly Americans can be more properly identified as a problem of fear
rather than of actual victimization. The article focuses on the
concerns that the elderly are removed from circumstances which allow for
social interaction. Policy implications are briefly discussed.

108. Liska, A., Lawrence, J., & Sanchirico, A. (1982). Fear of
      crime as a social fact. Social Forces, 60(3), 760-770.

Utilizing a national crime survey of 100,000 respondents 16 years of age
and older, this study sought to determine the actual level of fear of
criminal victimization. Two major questions were asked: opinions about
crime trends and how safe the respondents felt in and out of their
neighborhood during the day or at night. Special attention is given to
the elderly as a special category. Comprehensive statistics and numerous
tables are included. References are provided. Statistical analysis
incorporated with tables.

109. Normoyle, J. (1984). Age, physical design, and fear of
      crime among elderly public housing residents. Unpublished
      Dissertation, Loyola University of Chicago.

This study assesses and compares two explanations of fear of crime (age
homogeneity and environmental design) among a sample of 945 elderly
public housing residents in a secondary analysis of a national survey.
The study expanded on previous findings by independently assessing two
aspects of age homogeneity. Density, defined as the percent of the
housing population who are elderly, was distinguished from segregation
of elderly from nonelderly. Several explanations for fear of crime are
provided. However, a direct comparison indicated that age-homogeneity
factors were, in general, more important predictors of outcomes for
elderly than were physical design factors. The appendixes contain the
study instruments and an elaborate statistical analysis. A total of 99
references are provided.

110. Norton, L. & Courlander, M. (1983). Fear of crime among the
      elderly: the role of crime prevention programs. The
      Gerontologist, 22(4), 385-393.

This study examined the role of crime education programs on the fear of crime among 152 senior citizens. Project Safe (Seniors Against a Fearful Environment), a crime prevention program designed for elderly residents for six metropolitan regions in the eastern United States, consisted of educational presentations and increased patrol officer visibility. The assessment of this project found that respondents who were highly fearful were also highly security-conscious. A comprehensive scale development for fear of crime is included. Recommendations to reduce fear are most relevant for criminal justice agencies.

111. Ollenburger, J. C. (1981). Criminal victimization and fear of crime. Research on Aging, 3(2), 101–118.

A survey sample of 1,867 respondents are included in this research to examine the relationship between criminal victimization and age related characteristics, and to investigate the extent and reasons for high rates of fear of crime among the elderly. The survey included approximately 450 variables, 54 of which were related to crime, victimization, or fear of crime. Excellent source from which to draw baseline data. Comprehensive analysis procedures are presented including statistical analyses and tabular results. Excellent reference source.

112. Ortega, S. T. & Myles, J. L. (1987). Race and gender effects on fear of crime: an interactive model with age. Criminology, 25(1), 133–152.

In this research paper, multiple regression techniques are used to assess whether age, gender, and race interact in their effects on fear of crime. Factors associated with age, gender, and race that may influence fear of crime--perceived risk of victimization, actual exposure to crime, and the ability to cope with the consequences of victimization--are examined as they pertain to observed interaction effects. Findings are based on data from a 1979 survey of individuals residing in eight Chicago neighborhoods. Age is found to generally enhance rather than attenuate the effects of other culturally devalued positions. Tables and an extensive bibliography are provided.

113. Patterson, A. (1977). Environmental indicators - territorial behavior and fear of crime. Police Chief, 44(2), 42–45.

This research attempts to investigate the use of visual territorial displays on fear of personal assault and fear of property loss among elderly homeowners. Data were collected through unobtrusive observation of territorial markers and responses to a three-part questionnaire. The respondents were 157 homeowners age 65 and older, from predominantly white, middle-class communities in Pennsylvania. The results are discussed in the context of mastery of the environment by the elderly. References are included.

114. Pollack, L. M. & Patterson, A. H. (1980). Territoriality and fear of crime in elderly and non-elderly home owners. Journal of Social Psychology, 111 (June), 119–129.

Examines the relationship between territorial behavior and fear of crime

of elderly American homeowners, based on Patterson's two alternative
explanations. The respondents were 245 homeowners selected from several
predominately white, middle-class communities in Central Pennsylvania
communities. The research indicated that territorial behavior, as shown
by the presence of signs, barriers, and territorial markings are
significantly related to the homeowners level of fear. Although
Patterson's study gives support to the existence of a viable alternative
hypothesis, it prevents a defensible program with any confidence.

115.   Sherman, E. A., Newman, E. S. & Nelson, A. D. Patterns of age
        integration in public housing and the incidence and fears of
        crime among elderly tenants. In J. Goldsmith and S. S.
        Goldsmith (Eds.), Crime and the Elderly. Lexington,
        Massachusetts: D. C. Heath and Company.

This research concerns whether age-integrated housing or age-segregated
housing reduces fear of crime among the elderly. The results of a study
by the Institute of Gerontology (SUNY Albany) are presented. Its
purpose was to establish the effects of various living arrangements on
number and kinds of crime, fears and attitudes, and assess past and
present attempts to insure safety. Three living areas were studied: (1)
age-integrated, (2) age-segregated, and (3) mixed. The authors strongly
advocate age-segregated housing for the elderly. Implications and
policy alternatives are included. Two tables.

116.   Shotland, R., Hayward, S., Young, C., Signorella, M., Mindgall,
        K., Kennedy, J., Rovine, M. & Donowitz, E. (1979). Fear of crime
        and residential communities. Criminology, 17(1), 34-35.

This article analyzed two groups of women randomly selected to determine
the level of fear of victimization and the affects of the mass media on
the daily lives of the elderly. Three variables were perceived to cause
a fear of criminal victimization and a potential alteration of behavior
such as: (1) the type of crime committed, (2) the frequency of the
commission of the crime, and (3) the area in which the crime was
committed. Among the elderly different crimes may be differentially
feared.

117.   Smith, B. & Huff, C. R. (1982). Crime in the country: the
        vulnerability and victimization of rural citizens. Journal
        of Criminal Justice, 10(4), 271-282.

This study attempts to examine the crime patterns, measure the
victimization experiences, fears and perceptions of 11,262 people
located in a rural county in the midwest. In this study one-fourth of
the victimizations occurred outside the geographical limits of their
home county. Rural citizens feel less affected by increases in criminal
victimizations in their community, than in the country in general.
Numerous tables and references are included. Special attention given to
elderly victims.

118.   Sundeen, R. A., & Mathieu, J. T. (1976). The urban elderly:
        environments of fear. In J. Goldsmith and S. S. Goldsmith
        (Eds.), Crime and the Elderly. Lexington, Massachusetts: D. C.
        Heath and Company.

Reported here are the results of an exploratory study concerning the physical and social environments that increase or decrease the fear of crime among the elderly. Data was gathered from older persons living in nonpublic condominiums, apartments, and single-family residences in three types of communities in southern California: (1) core, (2) "slurb," (3) retirement. Attention was focused on four variables: (1) the degree of social support, (2) perception of safety in neighborhood, (3) fear of specific crimes, and (4) security precautions. Suggestions are provided as to reducing the fear of crime. Eight tables are included. References.

119. Sundeen, R. A. (1977). The fear of crime and urban elderly. In M. A. Young Rifai (Ed.), Justice and Older Americans. Lexington, Massachusetts: D. C. Heath and Company.

This article presents the results of a study conducted in Southern California. The data were collected from older persons living in nonpublic housing in three communities: a central city neighborhood, an urban municipality, and a retirement community. The purpose of the study was to assess the fear of crime and its consequences upon the elderly, rather than actual victimization. The specific criminal acts analyzed are burglary, robbery, and fraud. The results are also presented throughout the article in four major tables. Finally, generalizations are made for future policy formulation. References associated with fear are provided.

120. Sundeen, R. & Mathieu, J. (1976). The fear of crime and its consequences among elderly in three urban communities. The Gerontologist, 16(3), 211-219.

This study examines the findings of an investigation into the consequences of the fear of crime among 104 elderly persons in three communities in southern California. In the study, the fear of crime was measured by asking questions about specific crimes and situations. The primary concepts which were explored and compared were: (1) the degree of social support, (2) the perception of safety in the neighborhood, and (3) the fear of specific crimes. Finally, suggestions for security precautions were provided.

121. Toseland, R. W. (1982). Fear of crime: who is most vulnerable? Journal of Criminal Justice, 10(3), 199-209.

A national study of 1499 respondents, this article investigates the relationship of demographic, psychosocial, and crime related factors to the fear of crime. The independent variables considered for inclusion in the discriminate analysis included: sex, age, marital status, education, income, race, social class, persons living with respondent, size of place, health, helpfulness, trustworthiness, fairness, alienation, cynicism, life satisfaction, burglary, mugged, beaten, or threatened with a gun. A most comprehensive approach, 12 variables were found to contribute to respondent's fear. Statistical analysis procedures incorporates the variable of age very effectively.

122. Van Burne, D. P. (1976). Public housing security and the elderly: practice versus theory. In J. Goldsmith & S. Goldsmith (Eds.), Crime and the Elderly: Challenge and Response.

Lexington, Massachusetts: D. C. Heath.

A comparison is made between age-integrated and age-segregated housing projects on the basis of such factors as building security and elderly residents' feelings of safety. It is suggested that older adults living in age-segregated housing had more contacts with others, had less fear of crime, and used more informal crime prevention methods than elderly residents of age-integrated housing. The author concludes that age-segregated public housing seems to provide a social environment that seems to reduce the probability of elder victimization. Suggestions for social policy are included.

123.   Wiltz, C. J. (1982). Fear of crime, criminal victimization and elderly blacks. Phylon 43(4), 283-294.

Based on a non-random sample of 343 Black inner-city residents, the author attempts to develop a profile of the typical Black elderly crime victim. A useful comparison is made between victims and nonvictims. Conclusions are drawn that the elderly females have a greater fear of being victimized. A major determinant seems to be related to previous victimization experience and preceived probability of being victimized. Policy implications for law enforcement officers are presented. Future research agenda is suggested.

124.   Yin, P. P. (1982). Fear of crime as a problem for the elderly. Social Problems, 30(2), 240-245.

Utilizing a random sample of 1228 respondents, interviews were conducted to determine the global effects of how fear of crime impacts on the elderly. Twenty-eight percent of the sample belonged to what has been referred to as the "old-old," people aged 75 and over; the rest were between age 60 and 74. Fear of crime was measured by open-ended questions related to feelings of safety within the neighborhood. The dependent variables—neighborhood satisfaction, morale, and involuntary isolation were dichotomized. The article attempts to address the role that fear of crime plays in the everyday life of the elderly. Few policy implications to reduce fear of crime are presented.

125.   Yin, P. P. (1980). Fear of crime among the elderly: some issues and suggestions. Social Problems, 27(4), 492-504.

This article provides an excellent review of the literature on fear of crime among the elderly. Fear of crime is defined as "the amount of anxiety and concern that a person has of being a victim" and operationalized as whether surveyed respondents would name fear of crime as one of their three most serious personal problems. A conceptual framework within which to locate the strengths and weaknesses of previous research is included. An extensive discussion of the social determinants of fear of crime is presented. Consequences of the fear of crime which focus on mobilization behaviors, attitudes towards police, isolation, and well-being are offered. Bibliographical references are most comprehensive.

4   ELDER ABUSE AND NEGLECT

126.   Ambrogi, D., and London, C.   (1985).   Elder abuse laws: their
       implications for caregivers.   Generations,   10(1), 37–39.

This article examines the impact that mandatory reporting might have on
the current state of elderly abuse in the United States.   However, it is
stressed that without adequate support services mandatory reporting
alone will not be successful.   Causes of elderly abuse is briefly
discussed.   Inadequate societal response which includes the argument
that current punishment is often inappropriate for stressed caregivers
provides important social policy implications.

127.   Anderson, C. L.   (1981).   Abuse and neglect among the elderly.
       Journal of Gerontological Nursing, 7(2), 77–85.

Discussed in this article is the vulnerability of the elderly to
intentional or unintentional physical and emotional neglect and or
abuse, which may be self inflicted or inflicted by family or society.
Also examined is the health providers need to be alert for the signs and
symptoms of elderly abuse and or neglect and be aware of situations that
provoke potential abuse and or neglect so that appropriate interventions
can be utilized.   Continued progress made toward an improvement in care
of the elderly and a building of a sense of independence and autonomy
will benefit the elderly immensely in the present as well as in the
future.   Extensive references are provided.

128.   Bahr, R. T.   (1981).   The battered elderly: physical and
       psychological abuse.   Family and Community Health, 4(2), 61–69.

This article is a descriptive account of noninstitutional and
institutional abuse of the elderly.   Based on newspaper articles,
research reviews, and a case history, it is concluded that abuse is
sometimes camouflaged by symptoms which accompany the normal aging
process.   Legal definitions of abuse are discussed as well as the
importance of education in combating elder abuse.

129.   Beck, C. M. & Ferguson, D.   (1981).   Aged abuse.   Journal of
       Gerontological Nursing,   7(6), 333–36.

Examines the meaning of four types of elder abuse: violation of rights, material abuse, physical abuse, and psychological abuse. The article further explains the causes of elder abuse and emphasis is given to role theory and family systems theory as theoretical explanations. Sources of frustration and a scheme of denial and distortion are discussed.

130.   Beck, C. M. & Phillips, L. R.   (1983).   Abuse of the elderly.
       Journal of Gerontological Nursing, 9(2), 97–101.

This article presents a summary of the findings in the literature on elder abuse. The authors examine the effect that a frail elderly person has on family structure as well as the behavioral characteristics of a frail elderly person and his caretaker. A rationale is developed to explain elderly abuse of the confused family member. Contributes to the development of a model of elderly abuse.

131.   Block, M. R.   (1983).   Special problems and vulnerability
       of elderly women.   In J. I. Kosberg (Ed.), Abuse and
       Maltreatment of the Elderly; Causes and Interventions.
       Littleton, Massachusetts: John Wright, PSG, Inc.

This chapter examines victimization to which older women are more susceptible. A summary of previous research indicates that elderly women are much more vulnerable to certain types of crime and victimization than elderly men, particularly rape, purse snatching, elder abuse, burglary, and fraud. Fear of crime is reported to be an important issue with regard to the vulnerability of elderly women. Strategies for change are discussed in a limited fashion.

132.   Block, M. R., Davidson, J. L., and Sinnott, J. D.   (1979).
       Elder abuse and public policy.   In M. R. Block and J. D. Sinnott
       (Eds.), The Battered Elder Syndrome: An Exploratory Study
       College Park, Maryland: University of Maryland Center on Aging.

A comprehensive public policy system is suggested for solving the problem of elderly abuse. Utilizing a model of three levels of policy, the authors propose the establishment of a National Center on Elder Abuse and Neglect. Based on the notion that previous resources have been inadequate, it is suggested that the new center promote research, provide general information, and offer a variety of services in the area of intervention. Prevention strategies are also discussed.

133.   Bookin, D., & Dunkle, R. E.   (1985).   Elder abuse: issues for
       the practitioner.   Social Casework, 66(1), 3–12.

The authors describe the assignment of social workers to cases of abused elders. Significant problems are discussed which related not only to the nature of the problem but also to their own feelings, biases, and attitudes about violence and aging individuals. These problems are described as well as appropriate strategies for dealing with them. Case material is presented, and a table is provided that lists important variables and related avenues of investigation that can facilitate the accurate diagnosis and treatment of abused elderly clients. Implications of elder abuse for social work practice are also discussed.

134. Bragg, D. F., Kimsey, L. R., and Trabox, A. R. (1981). Abuse
      of the elderly: the hidden agenda. II. future research and
      remediation. Journal of American Geriatric Society, 29(11),
      503-507.

This article presents various solutions to the issue of elderly neglect
and abuse. The community-at-large, the medical community, and the legal
community are the major areas addressed which may lead to a reduction of
abuse and neglect. Recommendations for protecting older persons are
presented. Intervention strategies for the resolution of the problem
are recommended for the three sectors.

135. Callahan, J. M. (1982). Elder abuse programming--will it help
      the elderly? Urban and Social Change Review, 15(2), 15-19.

An emphasis is given to the development of public policy in relation to
elderly abuse and neglect. Five policy categories are discussed: issues
of definitions and expectations; problems with data and research; the
role of the media; supply side economics; and the potential
effectiveness of proposed solutions to the problem. Political, legal
and service solutions are examined. Further interventive
recommendations are provided.

136. Cazenave, N. A. (1983). Elder abuse and black americans:
      incidence, correlates, treatment, and prevention. In J. I.
      Kosberg (Ed.), Abuse and Maltreatment of the Elderly: Causes
      and Interventions. Littleton, Massachusetts: John Wright,
      PSG, Inc.

The major objective of this chapter focuses on how family violence is
affected by age and race. The author describes why the black elderly
are considered a special risk and the countervailing forces which works
against such abuse. Societal variables, individual characteristics and
precipitating factors are presented as significant factors in the
explanation of abuse among elderly black Americans. Intervention
strategies suggested to eliminate elderly abuse among blacks include:
attacking racism and economic exploitation, strengthening
family-kin-community networks, maintain health and independence and
reduce stressful environments and circumstances.

137. Champlin, L. (1982). The battered elderly. Geriatrics,
      37(1), 115-121.

A basic overview of several of the barriers to the prevention of elder
neglect and abuse are presented. Social, medical and legal issues
leading to limitations in intervention in cases of elderly abuse and
neglect are specifically examined. Illustrations and case histories are
utilized to highlight barriers. Conclusions relating to the political
arena are clearly provided.

138. Costa, J. J. (1984). Abuse of the elderly: a guide to
      resources and services. Lexington, Massachusetts: D. C.
      Heath and Company.

This resource book provides a broad overview to the problem of elder
abuse. The first section of the book provides the reader with six

articles previously published on the topic of elder victimization.
While informative, the major contribution of this book is the
comprehensive resources and services provided. This section includes
education and training materials (films, booklets, and pamphlets,
educational programs), programs in crime prevention for older persons,
and important organizations to contact. The book also contains a 75
page bibliography which is subject coded and includes references on
topics such as: victimization, physical abuse, mental abuse, fear,
prevention, reporting, and rehabilitation. A listing of relevant
journals is also provided.

139.   Crouse, J. S., Cobb, D. C., and Harris, B. B. (1981). Abuse
       and neglect of the elderly in Illinois: incidence and
       characteristics, legislation, and policy recommendations.
       Springfield, Illinois: Sangamon State University and Illinois
       Department on Aging.

This study stresses the development of a strategy to estimate the nature
and scope of elder neglect and abuse in the state of Illinois. Major
emphasis is given to legal research in order to identify basic legal
issues in intervention and legal provisions within Illinois. Based on
the random examination of seven Illinois communities, six types of elder
neglect and abuse are identified. In addition, three model service
systems are examined. The presence of elderly abuse and neglect is
projected to the nation as a whole.

140.   Douglas, R. L. and Hickey, T. (1983). Domestic neglect and
       abuse of the elderly: research findings and a systems
       perspective for service delivery planning. In J. I. Kosberg
       (Ed.), Abuse and Maltreatment of the Elderly; Causes and
       Interventions. Littleton, Massachusetts: John Wright, PSG, Inc.

This chapter reviews early evidence about the causes of neglect and
abuse of the elderly, and offers a systems analysis perspective of how
different service delivery efforts can be developed to reduce domestic
neglect and abuse. Several models are presented which portray the
elderly victim and their abusers. A discussion of the meaning of
maltreatment as well as domestic neglect and abuse causal hypotheses are
outlined. Strategies focusing on the development of interventive
response systems are also included.

141.   Douglas, R. L., and Ruby-Douglas, P. (1981). Domestic abuse
       and neglect of the elderly. In G. Braen (Ed.), Management of
       the physically and emotionally abused. San Diego, California:
       Macmillan.

A general article developed to increase the awareness of elderly abuse
and neglect found among family caregivers. The establishment of a
comprehensive elderly abuse identification model is viewed as essential.
Various ways the medical community and health care providers can be
educated to recognize abuse among the unique elderly population is a
major theme. A comprehensive profile and factors associated with abuse
in general is presented in the conclusions.

142.   _____. (1985). Elderly abuse: a national disgrace. report.
       U. S. House Select Committee on Aging and Subcommittee on

Health and Long-term Care. Washington, DC: U. S. Government
Printing Office.

This 64 page report on elder abuse in the U. S. presents data obtained
from questionnaires completed by state human services departments in
1984, plus case histories and other information. The report emphasized
such statistics as the fact that about 4% of the nation's elderly (1.1
million persons) may be victims of abuse, an increase of 100,000 abuse
cases annually since 1981. The majority of states have enacted adult
protective service laws to provide mandatory reporting of elder abuse.
However, only about 4.7% of an average state's protective services
budget goes for protection of the elderly. Tables and state resources
are included.

143. _____. (1981). Elder abuse and neglect - a guide for
     practitioners and policy makers. National Paralegal Institute,
     Mill Valley, CA.

This manual reviews current research on elderly abuse, presents
intervention strategies and protocols, discusses model delivery systems
and legislation, and provides information and materials for practitioner
training and public education. Information is based on four research
studies conducted in Massachusetts, Maryland, Michigan, and Ohio. These
studies give strong support to the impairment/dependency theory of the
etiology of elder abuse. Major theories on the causes of elderly abuse
are highlighted, including internal family dynamics and acute impairment
of the victim. Protocols for handling cases are reviewed. Developing
state and community response systems are given special attention.
Policy recommendations are provided. The 185 page document includes
case examples and extensive references.

144. Falcioni, D. (1982). Assessing the abused elderly. Journal
     of Gerontological Nursing, 8(4), 208-212.

The author develops a health history assessment instrument which takes
into consideration both family dynamics and the social structure of
relationships between the elderly and their caregivers. Based on a
literature review, definitions of abuse are discussed as well as causes
for abuse and characteristics of the abused and the abuser. An
assessment tool with pertinent illustrations provides the medical
community with a useful process to detect elder abuse. Recommendations
for intervention are also included.

145. Faulkner, L. R. (1982). Mandating the reporting of suspected
     cases of elder abuse: an inappropriate, ineffective, and ageist
     response to the abuse of older adults. Family Law Quarterly,
     16(1), 61-91.

This article addresses the dilemma of adopting a mandatory reporting
system for suspected elderly abuse cases. Developed to assist
policymakers, the author examines elder and child abuse studies for the
purpose of establishing a general policy proposal. Negative effects
such as a lack of services available to help solve the problem is
addressed. Agreement on the definition of elder abuse is essential to
the legislation for mandatory reporting laws for elder abuse as a basic

conclusion.

146. Ferguson, D., and Beck, C. M. (1983). H.A.L.F.: a tool to
      assess elder abuse within the family. Gerontological Nursing,
      4(5), 301-304.

This research identifies four factors as potential contributors to
abuse. These include: health status of the aged, family and aged
adult's attitude toward aging, living arrangements, and finances. A
data collection instrument containing 37 items distributed among these
four categories is presented. Utilizing a likert-type response, a
profile of actual abuse, elders at risk and unabused elders is provided.
A comprehensive family model focusing on intervention is outlined.
Policy strategies and implications for future research are both given
important attention.

147. Galbraith, M. W.   (1986). Elder abuse: perspectives on an
      emerging crisis. Kansas City, Kansas: Mid-America Congress
      on Aging.

Provides a collection of articles on theoretical issues, problems of
policy, practice, and research faced by the elder abuse field. Topics
of interest include: perceptions of adult caregivers, index for
assessing elder abuse, inpatient geropsychiatry programs, long-term care
ombudsman programs, volunteer programs, elder abuse statutes, and
techniques for problem resolution. This volume would be most useful to
practitioners who need an introduction to the field of elderly abuse.
The nine articles do not provide a systematic treatment of the field,
but do cover some of the basic issues in the field.

148. Galbraith, M. W., & Zdorkowski, R. T. (1985). A preliminary
      model of elder abuse. Free Inquiry in Creative Sociology,
      13(1), 79-108.

Based on the findings of 10 elder abuse surveys, the author's implicit
generalizations are presented in an interactionist model. The article
suggests that elder abuse is the predictable outcome of interactions
between and among elders' and abusers' characteristics. A list of
testable hypotheses is presented. Statistical analysis and implications
for scholars and practitioners are provided. Although elder abuse
surveys are not perfectly comparable, their findings are in general
agreement on many points, and the development of a theoretical model is
presented as plausible.

149. Gioglio, G. R., Blakemore, P. (1983). Elder Abuse in New
      Jersey: The Knowledge and Experience of Abuse Among Older
      New Jerseyans. Trenton: Youth and Family Services Division,
      New Jersey Human Services Division.

This study examines the nature and extent of abuse of senior citizens in
New Jersey. Interviews were conducted with a random sample of 342
elderly citizens. Approximately 57% of the abused elderly were 75 years
or older and 44 percent were over 80 years old. No incidents of abuse
of non-whites were reported. However, this may reflect the small sample
size. Recommendations are presented based on the findings.

150. Giordano, N. H., & Giordano, J. A. (1984). Elder abuse: a
      review of the literature. Social Work Case Work Journal,
      29(3), 232-236.

The authors examine the literature on elderly abuse in order to provide
a comprehensive view of the nature and extent of the problem, current
theoretical perspectives and the strategies for intervention. It is
concluded that the literature is inconsistent in presenting definition,
research methods, and underreporting of cases. Thus, caution should be
used in predicting the extent and nature of abuse. The need for a
national policy of elder abuse is stressed. Ways to coordinate such
programs through nationwide data collection and dissemination systems
are included. Excellent reference source.

151. Henton, J., Cate, R., & Emery, B. (1984). The dependent
      elderly: targets for abuse. In W. H. Quinn and G. A. Houston
      (Eds.), Independent Aging: Family and Social Systems
      Perspectives. Rockville, Maryland: Aspen Systems Corporation.

A comprehensive chapter that provides illustrations of the vulnerable
elderly. Types of abuse such as neglect, assault, misuse of finances
and property, and violation of rights are discussed. Factors related to
the occurrence of elder abuse which have been pinpointed by researchers
and theorists are examined. Family resources which promote independence
among the elderly are outlined. Conclusions are drawn which suggest
implications for public policy.

152. Hickey, T. & Douglas, R. L. (1981). Neglect and abuse of
      older family members: professionals perspectives and case
      experiences. Gerontologist, 21(2), 171-176.

A descriptive overview of neglect and abuse based on 228 respondents
representing five Michigan communities of socio-economic and ethnic
diversity is provided. Respondents rated case experiences of domestic
mistreatment on a five-point likert scale and were encouraged to
describe experiences in complete detail. While a general framework to
understand the reasons associated with elderly abuse is presented,
in-depth study of victims and their families is needed before
conclusions can be accurately drawn.

153. Hickey, T., & Douglas, R. L. (1981). Mistreatment of the
      elderly in the domestic setting: an exploratory study. American
      Journal of Public Health, 71(5), 500-507.

This article attempts to test four causes of elder abuse and to use
elder service professionals as resource persons for information on the
prevalence and dynamics of abuse in families caring for older persons.
A purposeful sample of 228 respondents providing direct services to the
elderly were interviewed. Explanations for abuse included such areas as
elder dependency, situational or life crisis, developmental disorders in
socialization, and factors in the social environment. Certain
recommendations in relation to protective services is included.

154. Hoback, J. (1981). New domestic violence studies: the battering
      of older women. MS, 10(1), 17.

A brief article on elder abuse in domestic settings. The author reviews
current data on the abuse of elderly women. Those interviewed include
researchers and counselors in the field. Case studies are provided.
Recommendations for the control of abuse include abused and protective
legislation for victims.

155. Hooyman, N. R. (1982). Mobilizing social networks to prevent
      elderly abuse. Physical and Occupational Therapy in
      Geriatrics, 2(2), 21-35.

This article outlines a proposed model for elder abuse prevention using
informal helping networks. The model examines how social agencies and
working professionals could mobilize, utilize or create the helping
networks in order to prevent elder abuse. A review of the literature is
a major component of this effort. Various helping networks are
identified. A practical approach with creative ideas.

156. Katz, K. D. (1979). Elder abuse. Journal of Family Law,
      18(4), 695-722.

Comprehensively reviews child abuse and elder abuse statutes. Based on
previous research, the author examines the definitions and causes of
elder abuse. Child abuse reporting statutes and the problems associated
with such statutes are reviewed. Applications are made from these
conclusions which provide policy implications for elderly abuse
reporting. Dilemmas related to this issue are addressed. Comprehensive
references relevant to the elder abuse and the legal system are
provided.

157. Kimsey, L. R., Tarbox, A. R., & Bragg, D. F. (1981). Abuse of
      the elderly: the hidden agenda of the caretakers and categories
      of abuse. Journal of American Geriatric Society, 29(1), 465-72.

This article provides a profile of caretakers and the types of neglect
and abuse elders may encounter. Issues relevant to both formal and
informal caretakers are addressed. Four types of abuse are identified
and illustrated. These include physical, psychological (conditions of
the facility, diet, grooming, benign neglect, verbal abuse and
infantilization), material abuse and fiscal abuse (embezzlement,
improper charges, improper record-keeping, mishandling of billing for
medication and medicaid fraud). An attempt is made to clarify issues
and guide future research in elder mistreatment.

158. King, N. (1983). Exploitation and abuse of elderly family
      members: an overview of the problem. Response, 6(2), 1-2,
      13-15.

Based on studies in Michigan, Massachusetts, Maryland and Ohio, this
research attempts to describe the nature and scope of elder abuse in
American society. While the literature does not provide conclusive
evidence for the incidence of elder abuse, a profile of the abuse and
abuser tends to be more easily identified. Basic causes of elder abuse
are discussed and a listing of states having mandatory reporting laws is
included.

159. Kosberg, J. I. (1983). The special vulnerability of elderly

parents. In J. I. Kosberg (Ed.), Abuse and Maltreatment of the
Elderly: Causes and Interventions. Littleton, Massachusetts:
John Wright, PSG, Inc.

This chapter examines reasons for the special vulnerability of the
elderly parents to abusive behavior by children and grandchildren.
Relevant literature on causes for elder abuse by immediate family
members is reviewed. Findings suggest that unique characteristics of
the elderly themselves, the abusing relative, the family system,
societal norms and presence of a community support system are important
variables associated with parental abuse. Recommendations for
prevention and treatment are also presented.

160. Krauskopf, J. M. & Burnett, M. E. (1983). The elderly person:
      when protection becomes abuse. Trail, 19(12), 60-67.

Stresses that while most of the trends to protect the elderly serve an
important purpose and are based upon humanistic motivations, the elderly
are often vulnerable to exploitation. There exists a growing potential
for damaging effects from either the improper use or the thoughtless use
of the statutes. Excellent discussions are provided on such topics as
protective devices, psychiatric dimensions, recovering damages for
misuse of protective devices, and malicious prosecution. Further
discusses the role the attorney can play in serving as an advocate for
the legal rights of the elderly in protecting their autonomy. Draws the
conclusion that aging itself does not automatically render a person
incapable of caring for personal needs or financial affairs.

161. Lau, E., & Kosberg, J. J. (1979). Abuse of the aged by
      informal care providers: practice and research issues. Aging,
      September/October, 10-15.

Examines various types of abuse of senior citizens by informal care
providers. An exploratory study of abusive behavior was taken to
determine the incidence and nature of abuse over a twelve-month period
from June 1977 through May 1978, at the Chronic Illness Center in
Cleveland, Ohio. Discussed in this article are numerous explanations or
theories for elderly abuse, and also various interventive strategies.
This article discusses further the problem of abuse which is currently a
neglected and hidden one which requires enough attention to initiate
large scale action in legislation and effective programming.

162. Liang, J. and Sengstock M. C. (1983). Personal crimes against
      the elderly. In J. I. Kosberg (Ed.), Abuse and Maltreatment of
      the Elderly: Causes and Interventions. Littleton,
      Massachusetts: John Wright, PSG, Inc.

In this chapter, the authors presents a systematic body of national
statistics about various aspects of personal crimes against the elderly.
Their research oriented discussion includes the risk of personal
victimization, the profile of the incident, the consequences of the
victimization, and the victim's reaction to crime. Statistical efforts
are made to view criminalization and victimization in a multivariate
context including the relationship between victimization and factors
such as individual and structural characteristics. Important policy
implications are also discussed.

163.   Moss, F. E. & Halamandaris, V. J. (1977).   <u>Too old too sick</u>
       <u>too bad: nursing homes in America</u> . Germantown, Maryland: Aspen
       Systems Corporation.

This book represents the underlying causes behind today's nursing home
problems.   Such topics as nursing home fear, nursing home abuses,
nursing home fires, profiteering, and various other substandard issues
are addressed.   The book is particularly valuable to nursing home
administrators since a special section analyzes each chapter in terms of
how they can do their job more effectively.   While the book may create
even more fear of nursing homes, it does address in a comprehensive
fashion the issues still facing the nursing home industry today.   A
special section on resources is provided.

164.   Oliveria, O. H. (1981).   Psychological abuse of the elderly.
       In Tennessee Conference: Abuse of Older persons, Knoxville,
       Tennessee, December 1980. <u>Conference proceedings.</u> Knoxville,
       Tennessee: School of Social Work, Office of Continuing Social
       Work Education, 115-122.

Special emphasis is given to the forms of psychological abuse inflicted
on the elderly not only by families, but also by society and
professional caregivers.   A brief review is provided of typical kinds of
psychological abuse with appropriate illustrations.   Psychological abuse
of the elderly is viewed as an overt or subtle verbal rejection of the
elderly which produces psychological stresses or trauma in the abused.
General suggestions for intervention are also addressed.

165.   Pedrick-Cornell, C., & Gelles, R. J. (1982).   Elder abuse:
       The status of current knowledge. <u>Journal of Family Relations,</u>
       31(3), 457-465.

The authors review the current literature on elder abuse and provide
recommendations for new directions for researchers and practitioners.
Three major goals are identified.   These include a report on the most
recent information on elder abuse, an analysis of the limitations of
current research and a proposed outline for new efforts in information
gathering and human service worker intervention.   New methods of
gathering abuse data are suggested.

166.   Pepper, C. D. (1983).   Frauds against the elderly.   In J. I.
       Kosberg (Ed.), <u>Abuse and Maltreatment of the Elderly: Causes and</u>
       <u>Interventions.</u> Littleton, Massachusetts: John Wright, PSG, Inc.

The author presents a descriptive overview of the fraudulent activities
committed against the elderly.   Numerous types of fraud such as work at
home schemes, securities, medical quackery, land fraud, funeral abuses
and Medicaid and Medicare fraud along with specific examples are
provided.   Various solutions at the local, state and national levels are
briefly examined.   The chapter provides excellent case histories from
the files of the House Select Committee on Aging.

167.   Phillips, L. R. (1983).   Elder abuse: what is it? who says
       so? <u>Journal of Geriatric Nursing,</u> 4(3), 167-70.

The article examines the subject of elder abuse in domestic settings and
stresses the complexity of the problem of abuse. Particular attention
is given to nurses who encounter potential abuse situations by reviewing
responses of public health nurses. Based on interviews with 34 public
health nurses who had participated in a study of 74 frail elderly
individuals ages 62 to 92, it was concluded that identifying abuse is an
extremely difficult task because most elder abuse cases are not examples
of definite battering. Suggestions are made as to how nurses can take a
more active role in elder abuse prevention.

168. Pillemer, K. (1985). The dangers of dependency: new findings
      on domestic violence against the elderly. Social Problems,
      33(2), 147-158.

Utilizing data from a case study of physical abuse of the elderly, this
article examines conflicting hypotheses emerging in the literature. One
such view is that the increased dependency of an older person causes
stress for relatives who then respond with physical violence. An
alternative hypothesis suggests that the increased dependency of the
abusive relative leads to maltreatment. The results of quantitative and
qualitative analyses seem consistent in that the elderly victims were
not likely to be more dependent, but were instead more likely to be
supporting the abuser. Extensive literature review is provided.
Important policy implications are included.

169. Pillemer, K. A. & Wolf, R. S. (1986). Elder abuse: conflict
      in the family. Dover, Massachusetts: Auburn House Publishing
      Company.

This edited book provides a state of the art on elder abuse and is aimed
primarily toward gerontologists, sociologists, psychologists, social
workers, psychotherapists, and policymakers. The book is organized into
three sections. Section one focuses on family contact in later life and
includes such topics as the burdens of the caregiver, intergenerational
relations, family reciprocity, and loving and hating one's elders. Part
two provides an extensive review of the empirical and theoretical
perspectives on elder abuse. Such issues as definition of elder
mistreatment, theoretical explanations and unresolved issues, and risk
factors are discussed. The final section stresses treatment and
prevention of family conflict and elder abuse. Important concepts in
this section include the development of intervention strategies, stress
reduction, home care resources, and environmental press. Excellent
resource book.

170. Pratt, C. C., Koval, J., Lloyd, S. (1983).   Service workers'
      responses to abuse of the elderly. Social Casework, 64(3),
      147-53.

This article examines physician and service providers responses to
hypothetical cases of elder abuse. An attempt is made to assess
intervention responses of social service providers and physicians to
hypothetical cases of elder abuse by family members. Based on four
vignettes representing hypothetical cases of elder abuse, it was found
that physicians were more likely than agency workers to refer elder
abuse cases to attorneys and clergy. Intervention strategies,
especially for the abuser, are also included.

171. Quinn, M. J. (1985). Elder abuse & neglect. <u>Generations,</u>
      10(2), 22-25.

This article, most relevant to practitioners, discusses the new
terminology, ambiguities, and problems in developing adequate
intervention programs for elder abuse and neglect. New methods for
adult protective services, physicians, home visiting nurses, home health
aides, housing counselors, lawyers, probate court judges, various social
program workers and law enforcement officers must be considered.
Special attention is given to the professions of social work and the
law, which must learn to interface with each other in a more efficient
manner. Thoughtful interventions that respect the rights of caregivers,
the rights of abused and neglected older adults, and the rights of
practitioners are offered as policy suggestions.

172. Quinn, J. J., & Tomita, S. K. (1986). <u>Elder abuse and neglect:</u>
      <u>causes, diagnosis, and intervention strategies.</u> New York, NY:
      Springer Publishing Company.

A most comprehensive overview of the current state of elderly abuse and
neglect. The book offers an interdisciplinary perspective as various
phases of elder abuse and neglect is applied to many professions. The
organization of the book provides the reader with a logical, systematic
course. The first section provides a basic overview of current research
findings and theoretical explanation and causes of elder abuse and
neglect. Case illustrations are utilized to provide a more vivid view
of various types of abuses. The second section of the book contains six
chapters focusing on abused diagnosis and intervention strategies. The
Elder Abuse Diagnosis and Intervention Model is described as one
alternative for practical application. The final section is aimed at
practice issues facing field workers. A bibliography and an appendixes
with extended information is provided.

173. Rathbone-McCuan, E. (1980). Elderly victims of family violence
      and neglect. <u>Social Casework,</u> 61(5), 296-304.

Discussed in this article is the possibility that many aged Americans
might be victims of family abuse, neglect, and other forms of violence.
Empirical data concerning intrafamily violence does not take into
account behavior that extends into the interaction between
multi-generational family units. This article futher examines the lack
of protection and assistance to aid the aged victim and an absence of
counseling for the abuser. Currently, no efforts have been made to
prevent this form of intrafamilial abuse, because the problem has gone
unrecognized.

174. Rathbone-McCuan, E., & Voyles, B. (1982). Case detection
      of abused elderly parents. <u>American Journal of Psychiatry,</u>
      139(2), 189-192.

Focuses on the elderly and the heavy price they pay as victims of
intrafamily abuse, neglect, and discrimination. Examined are strategies
to intervene and prevent cases of geriatric abuse with the family, two
major barriers must be overcome. Also, examined is the case detection

process to determine if the elderly is a victim and to identify the
abuser. Moreover, this article addresses the need to train persons to
aid the elderly in case detection of intrafamilial violence.

175. Regan, J. J. (1983). Protective Services for the elderly:
      benefit or threat. In J. I. Kosberg (Ed.), Abuse and Maltreat-
      ment of the Elderly: Causes and Interventions. Littleton,
      Massachusetts: John Wright, PSG, Inc.

Special emphasis is given to the delivery of services to elderly adults
at risk as well as the authority to intervene on behalf of the client.
The historical development of involuntary intervention and the direct
involvement of the legal system is the major focus. The chapter also
addresses the role state legislatures should play in revitalizing
mechanisms for persons needing assistance to appoint their protective
agents. Implications for social policy is thoughtfully incorporated.

176. Regan, J. J. (1978). Intervention through adult protective
      service programs. Gerontologist, 18(3), 250-54.

The article examines the forms of legal adult protective services and
provides an assessment of the degree to which the older person's rights
are preserved in the process of implementation. A review of the
literature and a case report form the basis of this effort. The
effectiveness of adult protective service laws is also discussed. These
protective service organizations are expected to provide services to the
elderly people to have the authority to intervene on the older persons
behalf. Guidelines are proposed for the purpose of altering the
guardianship law so that they might be more responsive to what is the
best interest of the older person.

177. Salend, E., Kane, R. A., Satz, M. (1984). Elder abuse
      reporting: limitations of statutes. Gerontologist, 24(1), 61-69.

Reviews 16 elder abuse reporting laws in the United States which were
passed between 1973 and 1980. Comparisons are made in the areas of
content and implementation, and overall effectiveness in protecting
victims of elder abuse. Telephone interviews were conducted with Adult
Protective Services supervisors in each state's largest city. Each of
the 16 states varied widely in purpose, coverage, registry requirements,
reporting requirements, immunity provisions, confidentiality provisions,
and mandated investigation or service components. No conclusions were
drawn regarding the effectiveness of elder abuse reporting law.

178. Sengstock M. C. & Barrett, S. (1984). Domestic abuse of the
      elderly. In J. Cambell & J. Humphreys (Eds.), Nursing Care
      of Victims of Family Violence. Restron, VA: Reston Publishing
      Company, 146-188.

Most comprehensive chapter which reviews some of the findings to date
concerning elder abuse and is based upon existing theories and previous
research in the field. Five major topics are discussed:
characteristics and frequency of domestic abuse of the aged;
characteristics of abused and abuser; proposed causes of elder abuse;
means used by agencies in identifying and serving abused aged; and
suggested nursing care for elder abuse victims. Numerous tables are

utilized to illustrate current abuse trends. A major section is provided
on theoretical causes of elder abuse which is most noteworthy.
Important policy implications can be found throughout the chapter. The
authors also report some original research. Extensive reference list.

179. Sengstock, M. C., Barrett, S., & Datwyler, M. M. (1981).
      Elderly multiple victims - more frequent than commonly thought?
      Paper presented at the 34th Annual Meeting of the Gerontological
      Society of America, Toronto, Canada.

This study utilized data from LEAA surveys to review the personal
victimization of older persons, incorporating the generally neglected
category of series victimization during a 6-month period. Analysis
showed that while personal series victimizations of the elderly were
relatively rare, failure to deal adequately with them resulted in an
underestimation of the prevalence of victimization of the elderly. A
re-estimate increased the frequency by about ten percent. The findings
suggest that further analysis of series incidents is needed to
understand their importance in the examination of victimization of the
elderly.

180. Sengstock M. C., Barrett, S., & Graham, R. (1984). Abused
      elders: victims of villians or of circumstances? _Journal of_
      Gerontological Social Work, 8(1-2), 101-111.

The article examines whether the families of the aged abuse victims
exhibit an inordinate number of stressful situations. Interviews were
conducted with 20 abuse victims who provided demographic information and
areas of disagreement and conflict in the family. The stress
experienced by the aged victims and their families were measured in
relation to three dimensions: the number of problems experienced, the
types and seriousness of the problems, and their scores on a cumulative
measure of the stressfulness of social situations. A large number of
highly stressful conditions were reported over the course of the year in
which the abuse was reported. Interventive strategies to reduce
stressful situations are presented.

181. Solomon, K. (1983). Victimization by health professionals and
      the psychologic response of the elderly. In J. I. Kosberg
      (Ed.), _Abuse and Maltreatment of the Elderly: Causes and_
      Interventions. Littleton, Massachusetts: John Wright, PSG, Inc.

The author describes several types of victimization and abuse suffered
by the elderly in America. Victimization factors such as economic,
role, attitudinal and physical are reviewed. The reinforcement of
victimization by the health professional is singled out. A lack of
awareness and stereotyping are mentioned as factors contributing to the
victimization by health workers. In addition, the psychologic mechanism
for coping with abuse as well as the effect of coping by the elderly is
acknowledged. A most comprehensive bibliography is included.

182. Stannard, C. I. (1973). Old folks and dirty work: the social
      conditions for patient abuse in a nursing home. _Social_
      Problems, 20(3), 229-342.

This article examines patient abuse in a small proprietary nursing home

utilizing data gathered through participant observation. Furthermore,
this article shows how daily working conditions of nurses in a
proprietary nursing home serve to keep them unaware of elderly patient
abuse. By the nurses following this daily working procedure, it opens
up ways for them to deny the existence of patient abuse when such a
claim is made by orderlies and aides. It is these same conditions that
makes patient abuse less visible, thus making it appear random and
infrequent, thereby covering up the fact that it appears to be a
patterned response of the aides and orderlies to their recurring
problems of controlling elderly patients.

183.   Steinmetz, S. K. (1983). Dependency, stress, and violence
       between middle-aged caregivers and their elderly. In J. I.
       Kosberg (Ed.), Abuse and Maltreatment of the Elderly: Causes
       and Interventions. Littleton, Massachusetts: John Wright, PSG,
       Inc.

This chapter addresses the problems experienced by both older persons
and their caregiving adult children as they confront the aging process
and elder care. The research reported here focused on the stresses,
conflicts, abuse and maltreatment experienced in families who cared for
an elderly parent. Based on an analysis of 77 interviews, the findings
indicates the relationship among dependency, stress and elder
mistreatment. The author presents an excellent review of the literature
and presents new terminology for dealing with this new problem.

184.   Steinmetz, S. K. & Amslen, D. J. (1983). Dependent elders,
       family stress, and abuse. In T. H. Brubaker (Ed.), Family
       Relationships in Later Life. Beverly Hills, California:
       Sage Publications, Inc.

This article investigates the relationship between dependency measured
by the frequency with which tasks or services need to be provided for
the elder, stress as perceived by the caregivers, and the abusive
techniques utilized to gain or maintain control. Utilizing a "snowball
technique," 104 respondents were interviewed by means of structured and
semistructured questions. High rates of dependency by the elderly were
linked to: household management, grooming, social-emotional needs,
financial management, mobility, and mental health needs. It was
concluded that dependency looks to stress. Conflict resolution
techniques are clearly presented and family policy issues discussed.

185.   Steinmetz, S. K. (1978). Battered parents. Society, 15,
       54-55.

Discusses several parallels between the battered child and battered
parent. Much of this battering takes the form of kindly neglect, due to
an inadequate knowledge about elderly caretaking. Thus, out of
necessity the child and elderly victim both recognize their dependency
on their abusing caretaker. Since the elderly are perceived to be a
nonproductive economic component of our society, their plight has not
stirred the public conscience to intervene and take up their protection
from abusive caretakers.

186.   Steinmetz, S. K. (1981). Elder abuse. Aging, 315(16), 6-10.

Based on in-depth structural interviews from 60 adult child caregivers or older persons, the author describes abuse of the elderly by their caregiver children. The findings suggest a number of significant problems in relation to elder abuse. Topics such as stigma and guilt, female vulnerability, elderly caregivers, and double demands of the sandwich generation are addressed. No statistical correlations are provided.

187. Steuer, J. L. (1983). Abuse of the physically disabled
      elderly. In J. I. Kosberg (Ed.), <u>Abuse and Maltreatment of the
      Elderly: Causes and Interventions.</u> Littleton, Massachusetts:
      John Wright, PSG, Inc.

This chapter discusses why the physically impaired elderly may be victims of elder abuse. Several disabling illnesses are reviewed and individual and family responses are examined in order to distinguish factors which may lead to abuse. While data is limited, certain stressors such as lack of social support, changes in homemaking and vocational activities, and overall changes in life style are suggested as factors associated with abuse of the physically disabled elderly. The major recommendation made is the fact that at risk families need to be identified and preventive intervention developed.

188. Steuer, J. & Austin, E. (1980). Family abuse of the elderly.
      <u>Journal of American Geriatric Society.</u> 28(8), 372-376.

This article describes the abuse of the disabled elderly by family members. Based on a study of 12 cases, elderly victims are identified and causes suggested. Possible methods of intervention and prevention are provided. Implications and suggestions for future research is an important focus of this study. Establishing guidelines for prevention which include public dissemination of resources available to the elderly is suggested.

189. Tomita, S. K. (1982). Detection and treatment of elderly
      abuse and neglect: A Protocol for health care professionals.
      <u>Physical and Occupational Therapy in Geriatrics,</u> 2(2), 37-51.

The article describes an elder abuse protocol which may be utilized in a number of environments by a variety of health care providers. A comprehensive description is provided on how physical and occupational therapists might use the detection instrument. Intervention strategies and a sample of the detection protocol used at Harborview Medical Center including specific instructions for administering the instrument are included.

5   CRIME PREVENTION PROGRAMS

190.   Anderson, L. M. & Davenport, D. O. (1981). Residential
       burglary prevention: seniors against crime and senior crime
       prevention officer program. Citizens Crime Prevention, Inc.,
       Burlingame, CA.

This extensive document (270 pages) states the goals, objectives, and
accomplishments for San Mateo County's (California) Seniors Against
Crime Program. The major purpose of the program is to increase senior
knowledge of crime prevention techniques and reduce their victimization.
The document describes the major phases of the program: (1) assessing
victimization rates and fear of crime, (2) distributing crime prevention
literature, (3) contacting 5,000 seniors in target areas four times a
week, (4) training senior volunteers to do home security inspections,
(5) presenting crime prevention programs to senior organizations, and
(6) the installation of home security kits. Extensive resources and
materials used in the Seniors Against Crime program are included in the
report.

191.   Arnone, W. (1974). Mobilizing the elderly in neighborhood
       anticrime programs. Aging, 236/237, 10-13.

Describes a senior citizens anti-crime network (SCAN) in two New York
city urban communities. A brief overview utilizing the community
development method is presented as a deterrence to criminal
victimization of the elderly. Through this program, the elderly are
inspired to take an initiative in deterring, shaping, and solidifying
the community in which they live to overcome criminal victimization.

192.   Baggett, S. & Ernst, M. (1977). From research to application:
       development of police and older adult training modules.
       Police Chief, 44(2), 51-54.

The development and operation of two training programs designed to
increase the reporting of crime by senior citizens is discussed. These
programs evolved directly from the findings of previous research which
reviewed the motivations for reporting vis-a-vis non-reporting by
various age groups. Based on a Dallas survey of 466 persons over the
age of 65, various reasons for non-reporting are discussed. As a

result, a two-hour in-service was designed which focused on increasing
the police officers' awareness of the special needs of older adults. A
second program was aimed at increasing the senior citizen's awareness of
their part in the criminal justice system and at correcting false
perception about the role of law enforcement.

193.   _____. (1980). Beating the burglar. National Retired
       Teachers Association, Washington, D.C.

This kit contains 80 color slides, a 15 minute audio-cassette, and
manual. The purpose of this slide and tape program is to provide older
persons with suggestions for protecting their home from burglary. A
dramatization of two young burglars is included. Advice is provided to
the elderly to remind them to: lock all windows, secure doors, store or
mark all valuables, and keeping the home looking occupied. A discussion
guide is provided.

194.   Beedle, S. (1982). Evaluation of the senior victims call-back
       program. Portland Bureau of Police Crime Prevention Detail,
       Portland, OR.

This research report evaluates the crime prevention program of the
Portland Police Bureau. The evaluation process examined how victims
felt about being contacted, what actions they took to prevent future
victimization, and what the subsequent victimization rate has been among
individuals contacted by the call-back program. During a 15-month
period, 2081 elderly victims were contacted. From this group, an
information and attitude survey was administered to a random sample of
132 respondents from the contacted group. Of this group 92 percent of
them indicated the call had a positive impact. Approximately two-thirds
believed that their chances of being victimized again were reduced by
the police contact. Survey instruments and tabular data are included.

195.   Beedle, S. & Strangier, J. (1980). Evaluation of the home
       security program. Portland Oregon Bureau of Police Crime
       Prevention Detail, Portland, OR.

Provides an evaluation of the Portland Home Security Program. This
program provides free locks and security hardware installation to
low-income homeowners. It was found that the program was quite
successful in delivering services to it's target population which
primarily included the elderly. Results of the Home Security Program
included a reduction of fear among participants, improved
police-community relations, and a reduction of the burglary rate.
Tables and the Home Security Program questionnaire and results are
appended.

196.   Blubaum, P. E. (1976). Maricopa county Arizona sheriff's
       department volunteer program. Police Chief, 43(2), 34-36.

The author describes a variety of volunteer programs which aid the
sheriff's department. In particular, senior citizens are one such group
which assist crime prevention programs. Some of the 47 organized
programs are comprised entirely of senior citizens. The author believes
that volunteer programs can utilize human resources from all segments of
the community, and the elderly are depicted as a very important

component of this crime prevention program.

197. Bishop, G. F., Klecka, W. R., Olendick, R. W., & Tuchfarber,
     A. J. (1979). United State Department of Housing and Urban
     Development, Washington, D.C.

The impact of four demonstration projects designed to prevent crime
against the elderly is evaluated. The evaluated programs were located
in New York City, Milwaukee, New Orleans, and Los Angeles. The
evaluation was based on two telephone surveys of the elderly population
living in the target neighborhoods and one survey of actual victims who
had been contacted by local communities. The evaluation was conducted
from the fall of 1977 to the fall of 1978. Results showed that efforts
at program visibility had moderate success. It was concluded that well
organized local programs were able to make an impact on their
communities. The report suggested that while elderly victimization
prevention programs are worthwhile, their success may be determined by
the staff chosen to run them. Extensive tables and appendixes
presenting research instruments and demographic characteristics of
public housing residents are included.

198. Bradley, W. W. (1976). Cass corridor safety for seniors
     project. Police Chief, 43(2), 43-45, 69.

The Detroit (MI) Multi-Phase Project was designed to provide a safe
environment for senior adults within a specific inner-city target area.
The project involves public education in the designated areas of crime
prevention, basic self defense, transportation services, a checkcashing
account phase, telephone reassurance, and overall safety education. One
basic purpose of the project is to serve as a model for other
communities.

199. Brostoff, P. M. (1972). Public Interest: Report No. 6 -
     beating up on the elderly: police, social work, crime. Aging
     and Human Development, 3(4), 319-322.

Stresses the needs for, and means of, reducing crime against the elderly
and providing them with assistance after a crime has been committed.
Provides an integrative approach in responding to crimes against the
elderly. A 1970 demonstration study in the District of Columbia,
Project Assist, is described. Important social policy issues for social
workers and police are presented. Several references are provided.

200. Brostoff, P. M. (1976). The police connection: a new way to
     get information and referral services to the elderly. In J.
     Goldsmith and S. S. Goldsmith (Eds.), Crime and the Elderly.
     Lexington, Massachusetts: D. C. Heath and Company.

This research concerns uniting an urban police department with a social
service agency to assist elderly victims of crime. Project Assist,
Washington, D.C., ran from October 1970 through April 1971, helping 220
clients. Referrals were made by walk-ins to the D. C. Police Dearment,
through police records, through other individuals who knew of someone in
need, and by other social service agencies. The functions of a referral
service are twofold: (1) to link people in need with the appropriate
agency to help them; and (2) assist in long-range community planning to

discover gaps and duplication of service. The functions of the police
are discussed as well. Three case studies and policy implications are
provided.

201.   Buford, A. D. (1977). Nonlawyer delivery of legal services.
        In M. A. Rifai (Ed.), Justice and Older Americans, Lexington,
        MA:D. C. Heath and Company.

The training and qualifications of paralegal personnel and the
law-related services that paralegals and other nonlawyers can provide
for elderly persons are discussed. While paralegals cannot practice
law, they can assist in research, drafting documents, gathering facts,
investigating, assisting in preparation for litigation, and performing
other tasks formally completed by attorneys. Paralegal programs for the
elderly which offer employment opportunities to older persons and extend
services to elderly people who cannot retain an attorney are dscussed.

202.   Cairns, W. L. (1977). Senior citizen turn cop spotters.
        Police Chief, 44(2) 34-37.

In July, 1976, 2,200 senior citizens and members of the Mansfield, Ohio,
Auxiliary Police Organization came together to aid police in watching
neighborhoods for crime and suspicious activity. Since the
implementation of the Neighborhood Watch Program among Mansfield's
elderly, crime has dropped; and police officials are unable to explain
why. As a result of the lower crime rate, senior citizens volunteers in
Mansfield, have generated a new enthusiasm on the part of the public to
assist the police in the fight against crime.

203.   _____ . (1980). Call the next witness. National Retired
        Teachers Association, Washington, D. C.

Call the Next Witness is a kit which contains seventy-two color slides,
a 30 minute audio-cassette, and manual. The major purpose of this
presentation is to provide information on how to effectively serve as a
courtroom witness. Witnesses are advised to visit the court room prior
to their appearance, to dress with restraint, and to remember to bring
the subpoena or summons to the trial. Included with the program are a
list of equipment needed for a presentation, a discussion guide for
program moderators, and a typed script of the taped narrative.

204.   _____ . (1979). Cleveland, Ohio, elderly seek the improbable:
        their own cops. Criminal Justice and the Elderly. (Summer
        1979), 5-10.

This article describes the efforts of a senior citizen coalition found
in Cleveland, Ohio, and comprised of approximately 70 elderly-serving
organizations, to get special police protection for the elderly. This
request met with considerable resistance from the criminal justice
community. The rationale provided in this article focuses on the
utility of special detective squads and the problems of appropriate
division of responsibility among team members if an investigation is
warranted. Some seem to argue the point that special units would
promote an increased trust of criminal justice agencies. Others felt
benefits of special units are marginal and costs are prohibitive.

205. Center, L. J. (1979). Anti-crime programs for the elderly - a
      summary evaluation report. National Council of Senior Citizens
      Criminal Justice and the Elderly Program, Washington, D. C.

This document summarizes the findings of the process and impact
evaluations of seven demonstration projects which began in 1977 and were
designed to prevent crime against the elderly and assist elderly crime
victims. The seven projects were developed to help the elderly avoid
victimization, reestablish social networks and strengthen neighborhoods,
aid elderly victims, and expand public awareness of the crime-against
the elderly problem. Evaluations from the projects concluded that crime
prevention training should be organized and planned according to a
number of factors, including the neighborhood type and identity of the
audience. Television was found to be an important means of
disseminating information about crime and advisory committees were found
to be an effective process of obtaining feedback from the elderly.

206. Center, L. J. (1979). Anti-crime techniques for elderly
      apartment dwellers organizing strategies and legal remedies.
      Criminal Justice and the Elderly, Washington, D. C.

This monograph is based on research and experiences with elderly
anti-crime programs and fully addresses the crime-related needs and
programs of elderly apartment dwellers in inner cities. The document is
designed primarily for staffs of crime prevention projects. Community
crime prevention measures discussed include: organizing residents to
fight crime through tenant patrols, alarm systems or buddy buzzers,
whistle or airhorn distributions, telephone assurance, escort services,
and other strategies. Discussion also focuses on measures to increase
physical security in apartments. Examples of home security survey
checklists and other data from several crime prevention programs are
attached.

207. Center, L. J. (1982). Victim assistance for the elderly.
      Victimology, 5(2-4), 374-390.

This article describes in detail the assistance that community agencies
and the police should provide when victimization occurs. A national
demonstration program indicated that the elderly need counseling,
medical and financial help, replacement of lost documents,
transportation, and other services. It was concluded that a speedy
referral process is an important prerequisite for crisis intervention
counseling. Ways to get in touch with the elderly and appropriate
organization for service delivery to elderly clients is included.
Policy implications are implied. Several assistance programs are
reviewed.

208. _____. (1982). Crime and the elderly - New Jersey. Hearing
      Before the House Select Committee on Aging, Englewood, New
      Jersey.

This sixty-six page field report provided testimony on the
vulnerabilities of the elderly to participate in crimes and the means
for countering such crimes and reducing their consequences for the
elderly. Statistics provided evidence that aged persons 65 years or
older are less likely to be victims of every category of crime except

purse snatching and pickpocketing. However, this particular hearing did
report that the consequences of victimization are greater for the
elderly, since physical injuries are slower to heal; the psychological
stresses are much greater; and economic losses are more difficult to
recoup. Various measures for countering these crimes are suggested.
Policy implications are suggested.

209. _____. (1979). Crime and the elderly – training guide.
     International Association of Chiefs of Police Bureau of
     Operations and Research, Gaithersburg, MD.

Typical crimes committed against the elderly are discussed, and steps
police can take to assist elderly victims are outlined. The major
contention of this report is that police contacts with senior citizens
who have been criminally victimized require special thought and action
based on an understanding of the plight of the elderly victim.
Recommendations regarding ways police can help reduce elderly
victimization are included. Specifically, the police can assist elderly
victims by using communications skills that comfort the victims,
clarifying the assistance that can be realistically expected, and
assuring them of the full cooperation of the police. Both verbal and
nonverbal techniques for communicating with the elderly are outlined,
and suggestions are made on how to conduct interviews with older victims
or witnesses.

210. _____. (1981). Crime and the elderly – what your community
     can do – hearing before the senate special committee on aging,
     Albuquerque, New Mexico. U.S. Congress Senate Special Committee
     on Aging, Washington, DC.

The purpose of this extensive report was to gather information to assist
the Senate in evaluating the various Federal programs directed at
helping senior citizens and to determine the efficiency of the Older
Americans Act, which was under consideration for reauthorization.
Representatives of the New Mexico Criminal Justice Department, the New
Mexico State Police Department, the American Association of Retired
Persons, the Office of Senior Affairs for Albuquerque, and the Rio
Grande Elderly Crime Stoppers of Alburquerque presented testimony before
the committee. Major topics included senior crime stopping techniques,
citizen awareness of the problem, fear of crime, criminal methods, and
geographic distributions of crime in New Mexico. Letters, newspapers
articles, and additional statements are included.

211. _____. (1981). Crime and the elderly – what you can do. U.S.
     Congress Senate Special Committee on Aging, Washington, DC.

This twenty–six page document identifies those crime problems which are
the most serious threats to the elderly and gives practical and tested
advice on what the elderly can do to reduce risks of becoming a crime
victim and help prevent crime in their neighborhoods. Steps for
reducing risk of being victimized at home cover such topics as: locks,
doors, windows, lighting, prolonged absences, insurance information, and
landscaping. Steps for reducing victimization are also presented for
various con games, including buying by mail and at the door, home
repairs, signing your name, buying on credit, healthcures and health
machines, health insurance, and glasses and hearing aids. Information is

provided on the action one should take if victimization actually occurs. Advice is also provided on how to get more information on reducing crime against the elderly.

212.   _____. (1980). Crime prevention for senior citizens - an action guide. Walter P. Reuther Senior Centers, Detroit, MI.

This packet of brochures provides crime prevention information for senior citizens on topics such as home locks, car and home protection, identifying property against theft, personal safety and other topics. These publications are useful for placement at senior citizen's centers or public housing facilities for the elderly. Also included in the packet is a crime prevention survey, guide for use of the action guides, charts and useful illustrations.

213.   Culp, M. W., & Calvin, M. L. (1977). Victim service programs. In M. A. Young Rifai (Ed.), Justice and Older Americans. Lexington, Massachusetts: D.C. Heath and Company.

This article critiques the criminal justice system as an impersonal, dehumanizing experience for an elderly crime victim. Basic criteria are offered for the formulation of an effective victim assistance program. They are: case program information, community resource identification and referral, obtaining property release, restitution, and victim decision making. Finally, elderly victim assistance programs in Kansas City, Missouri, and Alameda County, California, are highlighted.

214.   Davis, L. J. & Brady, E. M. (1979). Rape and older women: a guide to prevention and protection. Philadelphia Geriatric Center, Philadelphia, PA.

This comprehensive document serves as an important guide to prevent rape and to reduce fear of assaults among elderly women. The discussion of this guide centers on the process of aging, the vulnerability of older women, and the impact of rape on elderly female victims. The study reports that although older women are not raped as frequently as younger females, they are profoundly affected by a constant fear of becoming victims. The guide suggests specific avoidance behaviors that older women can practice to reduce rape and the fear of rape. Resources from education and training programs are provided for those in need of audiovisual and written information. Additional information on existing prevention and crisis intervention programs is also included. Statistical data, a glossary, and a list of references are provided.

215.   D'Angelo, S. (1977). Senior home security program. Police Chief, 44(2), 60-61.

This article illustrates the extreme hardships that burglaries can have on senior citizens. The author outlines the formation of a program, funded by the National Council on Aging, to help senior citizens take physical steps to make their homes more safe. The article also explains that the funding was used to improve and repair senior citizen centers, and to help the elderly in other ways.

216.   Dudovitz, N. S. (1985). The least restrictive alternative. Generations, 10(2), 39-41.

This brief article discusses issues related to guardians and civil
rights of the elderly. Current civil rights law prevents public
guardians from having absolute power over frail elders assigned to them.
Some have suggested the creation of new legal procedures such as
protective services or expanded durable powers of attorney as the answer
to meeting the needs of the vulnerable elderly. While laws require that
all guardians, public and private, act in the best interest of the
elderly, this is virtually unenforceable standard. Important policy
implications are suggested. A case study is included. No references.

217.   Friedman, D. M. (1976). A service model for elderly crime
       victims. In J. Goldsmith and S. S. Goldsmith (Eds.), Crime and
       the Elderly. Lexington, Massachusetts: D. C. Heath and Company.

To assist elderly victims of crime, a "service" model of assistance is
proposed. The pilot program, the Crime Victims Service Center, was
begun in the Bronx, New York. The program is government-sponsored, and
is administered by the Center for the Study of Social Intervention,
Department of Psychiatry of Albert Einstein College of Medicine. Two
basic components are discussed: (1) human service which includes direct
counseling and referral services; and (2) prevention. Three service
gaps identified are protection, legal services, and immediate financial
assistance to crime victims. Interdependence of components are
stressed. Several case studies are presented.

218.   _____. (1980). Florida's plan to reduce crime against the
       elderly. Florida Bureau of Criminal Justice Assistance,
       Tallahassee, FL.

This report focuses on ways to reduce fear of crime as well as crime
itself in the state of Florida. The report referred to as Florida's
1980 Plan list 20 priorities for implementation of special program to
reduce crime against the elderly. The priorities include funding crime
prevention programs, collecting victimization data, researching causes
for elderly victimization, developing compensation programs for elderly
victims, distributing crime prevention information, and teaching the
elderly crime prevention techniques. Each priority is preceded by a
brief problem statement. The problem statement is followed by a
strategy for implementation. The priorities are ranked according to
their importance concerning the severity of the problem. Tables,
charts, and extensive information sources are incuded.

219.   _____. (1980). Fraud and other con games. National Retired
       Teachers Association, Washington, DC.

This kit contains 113 color slides, a 15 minute audio-cassette and a
manual. A slide and tape program for older persons, this program
focuses on swindles which are frequently committed against the elderly.
Among the con games dramatized are the bank examiner, the pigeon drop,
the home repairman, the city inspector, the contract man, and the
retailer's bait and switch trick. The kit encourages the elderly to be
suspicious of persons who approach them about money withdrawal, etc.
Adequate support information is provided.

220.   Goldsmith, J. (1975). Community crime prevention and the

elderly - a segmental aproach.   Crime Prevention Review,
2(4), 17-24.

This article offers a basic overview of the utilization of segmental
crime prevention based on the elderly potential victim population.   A
comparison is made between the base of the potential victim population
and the specific targeted crimes which are of particular concern to the
elderly segment.   Also provides comprehensive review of the special
nature of crimes against the elderly.

221. Goldstone, R. (1977).   Crime victims strike back.   Police
      Chief, 44:26-28, 86.

Describes a new senior citizen crime prevention program developed with
the assistance of the W.I.S.E. team.   This team is made up of senior
citizens who present the program to other senior citizens.   The W.I.S.E.
program is three-fold in nature.   The first part deals with personal
safety, home security, and bus and auto safety.   Secondly, the program
deals with consumer fraud and bunco.   Thirdly, the program is conceived
of as a "hardware" program.   During the five and a half months of 1976
when the personal safety educational program was given, it covered
twenty-five sites and reached over fifteen hundred senior citizens.

222. Gross, P. (1977).   Summary report: crime, safety, and the
      senior citizen.   Police Chief, 44(2), 18-26.

Summarizes the activities of the Model Project on Aging conducted by the
International Association of Chiefs of Police.   This model project also
presents information on agencies and programs serving the elderly.
Included in this article is a sample survey instrument which was
developed to assess the attitudes and problems of senior citizens and
the impact of crime on their lives.

223. Gross, P. (1977).   Crime, safety and the senior citizen.
      Police Chief, 44(2), 18-26.

This article utilizes numerous surveys and case studies to develop
programs for reducing the victimization of the elderly and for
incorporating the vast resources of our senior population into police
department service.   A model project on aging, was funded by the
Administration on Aging and the U.S. Department of Health, Education,
and Welfare; to cope with the problems of senior citizen safety and to
enhance the interrelationship between the senior population and law
enforcement agencies.   The achievement of these ojectives will result
not only in employment opportunities for the older American but, more
importantly, will establish an atmosphere of security to enable senior
individuals to lead a life free from fear or victimization.   A list of
resource organizations is included.

224. Kelly, D. (1979).   Stockton police department's senior
      citizen's assistance program.   Crime Prevention Review,
      6(3), 16-20.

The Stockton Police Department's assistance program for senior citizens
is presented.   The program consists of 8 weeks of classroom training.
Information on services available to senior citizens through the Area

Agency on Aging is included. A brief description of the program is
provided. While no data have been gathered to test the program's
effectiveness, it is assumed by the author that acquiring new crime
prevention information will reduce a participant's probability of
victimization.

225. Leeds, M. (1977). Residential security techniques. In
      M. A. Young Rifai (Ed.), Justice and Older Americans.
      Lexington, Massachusetts: D. C. Heath and Company.

Three theoretical views are presented in the opening pages as to how
public housing projects may be made safer. The elderly are very often
targeted for experimenting with new designs. These theoretical concepts
are: "defensible space" - Oscar Newman; "turf reclamation" - Seymour
Rosenthal; and planning - Richard Gardner. Results from an empirical
study assessing the crime problem are presented. Included in this
discussion are elaborate diagrams and tables of the results. Finally,
some suggestions are made to increase safety for public housing
residents.

226. McGowan, R. H. (1977). The implementation of a victim
      assistance team program for the elderly. Our senior citizens:
      now a way to help. Police Chief, 44:54-55.

Utilized are two training programs designed to increase the reporting of
crime by senior citizens, by increasing the awareness of police and the
criminal justice system in Pasadena, California. This program is just
one of many attempts to involve senior citizens in the fight against
crime. It is the hope of this project that an increased understanding
on the part of law enforcement and citizens alike can have a major
impact in the prevention and resolution of crime in our society. This
article states an interest and concern that is indicative of the need
for such community involvement projects and marks a dramatic and
positive change for the senior citizen community.

227. Miller, C. (1977). Elderly crime prevention: a blueprint for
      action. Police Chief, 44(2), 64-66.

Guidelines for establishing operational programs concerned with
preventing crime against senior citizens are discussed. The author
includes a list and description of the steps to follow in organizing a
crime prevention program. Projects that have been successful are also
presented. The author concludes with the premise that efforts should be
directed toward actually interfacing with the aged and reducing their
fear and making them less likely to be victimized.

228. Miller, M. & Willis, R. L. (1976). Senior citizen crime
      prevention program. Police Chief, 43(2), 16-17.

This article describes a senior citizen volunteer program in Cottage
Grove, Oregon. The major focus of the program is to prevent crime
against senior citizens by conducting home visits. The purposes of
these visits are to make personal property (operation identification);
inspect door locks, window latches, and other home security devices; and
to inform the senior citizen as to the local, state, and federal
agencies that are available to serve them.

229. Nitzberg, R. (1978). Guide to training materials in criminal
      justice and the elderly. Criminal Justice and the Elderly,
      Washington, D. C.

This 74 page document is an annotated guide to previous literature,
training programs, and films which can be utilized for the purpose of
prevention and victim compensated training programs for the elderly.
The materials include information and training programs produced from
1971 to 1978. A sample of informative topics include: consumer fraud,
personal and property protection, community organizing, crisis
intervention, self-defense, coping with crime, and neighborhood and
group action. The printed materials are listed alphabetically by author
and the films alphabetically by title. A list of other bibliographies
of training materials is also included.

230. Nitzberg, R. (1979). Crime prevention for senior citizens:
      trainer's manual. Criminal Justice and the Elderly, Washington,
      D. C.

This manual is primarily designed to teach crime prevention techniques
to senior citizens and describes the structure and content of crime
prevention training sessions for the elderly. The manual is based on
two years of research during which training, films, literature, and
brochures on elderly victimization were reviewed. The manual divides
the topic of crime prevention education into five different topical
areas: (1) becoming aware of crime, (2) protecting yourself on the
street, (3) protecting your property, (4) consumer fraud and con games,
and (5) collective action. To facilitate the use of a variety of
techniques to teach the topics, five modules for each of the five topics
are included. Each module utilizes a different technique. Each module
also provides detailed instructions on how to use the technique
including information on time required, group size, instructional
objectives, equipment and materials.

231. _____. (1980). Outsmarting crime: an older person's guide to
      safer living. New York, NY: Harper and Row.

An educational training kit containing 80 color slides with an audio
cassette. The guide provides encouragement for the elderly to assume a
more active role in preventing crime. The focus of the slide
presentation includes both personal and residential crime prevention and
deterrence. Various crime prevention techniques are emphasized to curb
nonviolent crime because statistics indicate that the elderly are more
often the victims of burglary.

232. _____. (1978). Pasadena police banking new crime fight will
      help senior citizens. Crime Control Digest, 12:4-6.

Examined in this article is the Senior Citizens Against Theft project in
Pasadena, California. S.C.A.T. is an adaptation of the U.S. Treasury
Department's direct deposit campaign which they have been promoting
since 1976. The S.C.A.T. program is supposedly one of the best crime
resistance tools ever created, especially in the elderly community,
which depends so heavily upon the monthly federal payments and benefits.
It reduces opportunities for crime, since the criminal will have a much
more difficult time spending stolen checks and money orders, the profit

motive for crime is reduced.

233.   Persico, J. E. & Sunderland, G.   (1985).   Keeping out of
       crime's way.   AARP Books, Dept. BF5, 400 S. Edward St., Mount
       Prospect, IL.   60056.

A comprehensive crime prevention book which stresses crime intervention
strategies.   The book demonstrates how to reduce victimization as well
as being a valuable resource guide/training manual for police crime
prevention officers.   The book is also a useful resource and reference
tool for neighborhood crime prevention groups, such as neighborhood
watch and senior citizen volunteer security patrol organizations.   Most
useful listing of community resources is provided.

234.   Piland, R.   (1977).   Surviving old age: criminal justice
       response to the problem.   In M. A. Young Rifai (Ed.), Justice
       and Older Americans.   Lexington, Massachusetts: D. C. Heath
       and Company.

This article highlights how a number of local, state, and federal social
service agencies have assisted in creating crime prevention programs for
the elderly.   The elderly, as a result of these programs, have been
educated about crimes such as residential burglary, commercial burglary,
robbery, rape, shoplifting, and theft.   Heavy emphasis is also placed on
the education and cooperation of law enforcement personnel.   Finally,
the results of a vicimization study are presented in an itemized list
form.

235.   _____.   (1979).   Protecting the elderly from criminal
       victimization and providing services to elderly victims of
       crime.   New York State Division of Criminal Justice Services
       Planning Unit, Albany, New York.

This ninety-three page document is an effort to protect the elderly from
criminal victimization and to provide services to those who have been
victims of crimes.   A comprehensive profile of the elderly in New York
and the extent of their victimization is provided.   Statewide, local and
federal efforts to address the problem of elderly victimization are
examined.   Efforts and activities of the New York Division of Criminal
Justice Services are explored, such as data collection, the development
of the comprehensive crime control plan, and funding of crime prevention
and victim assistance programs.   A list of projects funded by the crime
control planning board to assist the elderly and a summary table of
initiatives by county offices for the aging to protect the elderly are
included.

236.   Rifai, M. Y.   (1977).   Implications for crime prevention: the
       response of the older adult to criminal victimization.   The
       Police Chief, 44(2), 48-50.

Based on 300 case reviews from police records and from a random sample
of 500 adults over the age of 60, this article focuses on elderly
individuals who initiated increased security measures to deter or
protect against criminal victimization.   Concerns regarding crime are
characterized in three dimensions: specific situation and area concerns,
anxieties about other people, and generalized anxiety.

237. Ritchey, L. W. (1977). Crime: can the older adult do anything
      about it? Police Chief, 44(2), 56-57.

A survey utilizing elderly respondents was conducted in Salem, Oregon,
and a three country surrounding area. The research questionnaire was
directed at three areas of concern for senior citizens: (1) income
maintenance, (2) medical/financial, and (3) criminal activity. Examined
are the effects of victimization suffered by a senior citizen after
coming into contact with a crime situation. The article further states
that until police are sensitized to the problems of the elderly and
begin working toward bridging the gap through understanding, the
problems will continue to exist.

238. Sardino, T. J. (1977). Syracuse police department's senior
      citizen recognition program. Police Chief, 44(2), 16.

After a brief review of the special problems of the elderly with respect
to crime victimization, the author describes two Syracuse Police
Department programs designed to recognize and aid elderly citizens. One
such program involves a police officer whose primary duty is to review
all crime reports, determine who the elderly victims are, and to provide
them with a follow-up visit. The second program, called the Senior
Citizen Recognition Program, provides part-time jobs for two senior
citizens and provides valid identification cards for all Syracuse senior
citizens.

239. Schack, S. & Frank, R. S. (1978). Police service delivery
      to the elderly. American Academy of Political and Social
      Science, 43 (July), 81-95.

This article describes an extensive survey conducted in two large
American cities. The major goal of the survey is to assess elderly
citizen attitudes toward police services. All respondents were 60 years
of age or older and were selected by random probability sampling. A
total of 913 interviews were conducted, divided equally between the two
cities. The elderly report a positive attitude toward the police.
Those who have utilized the police before tended to have less positive
attitudes toward the quality of police services they have received or
expect to receive. Recommendations are proposed to improve police
service delivery to the elderly.

240. Schneider, A. L., & Schneider, P. R. (1977). An introductory
      guide to evaluation of victim assistance programs for project
      directors. In M. A. Young Rifai (Ed.), Justice and Older
      Americans. Lexington, Massachusetts: D. C. Heath and Company.

This article serves as a guide, or checklist, for project directors of
victim assistance programs in order to evaluate their programs.
Basically, the guide centers on four issues: (1) identify the different
types of evaluation procedures and what might be learned from each, (2)
decide what types of procedure is needed for a particular agency and how
reliable the results will be, (3) determine what the information will be
used for, (4) choose an evaluation plan that is right for the particular
program. In general, this article takes a common-sense approach to the
evaluation process.

241. Scroogs, A. (1977). Project concern – cooperative program
      focuses on youth and elderly victims. Police Chief , 44(4),
      58–59.

A description is provided of a crime prevention program in St.
Petersburg, Florida, which was jointly sponsored by local government and
a volunteer organization to reduce crime and prevent unfounded fears of
crime in two target areas. The areas chosen included 11 census tracts
which are experiencing an increase in crime and a rising fear of crime.
Partial statistics for the first year of operation indicate that Project
Concern's target and walk-in social service activities may be partially
responsible for a decreasing crime rate.

242. Sengstock, M. C. & Liang, J. (1979). Responses of the elderly
      to criminal victimization. Paper presented at the American
      Society of Criminology, Philadelphia, PA.

Data is presented which focuses on the responses of elderly persons to
the experience of being a victim of personal crime. Based on a
literature review of the elderly's attitudes toward reporting crimes,
the elderly appear to be reluctant to report a crime to the police
because of fear of retaliation, confusion and embarrassment following
the incident, and excessive expense. The authors also discuss the role
fear plays in the curtailment of social activities as well as the
passage image based on a lack of resistance on the part of the elderly
victim. Utilizing data from LEAA's 1976 National Crime Survey on
responses by victims 60 years and older, it was reported that only 11
percent of all elderly victims were subjected to personal crimes.
However, this type of attack is most feared and about half the victims
did not respond directly to the offender, while only 20 percent
confronted the offender through physical force or reasoning. Tables and
29 references are included.

243. Smith, R. J. (1979). Crime against the elderly: implications
      for policymakers and practitioners. International
      Federation on Aging, Washington, D.C.

This 61 page document characterizes criminal victimization of the
elderly and suggests effective policy analysis to be implemented through
programs for immediate change. The monograph argues the fact that the
statistics fail to document the extend of crime against the elderly
because crimes to which they are especially vulnerable, such as
institutional abuse or neglect, consumer fraud, medical quackery, and
even purse snatching fall outside the reported categories of serious
crimes. It is suggested that attention should be given toward developing
a full service policing program and a systems approach to integrating
victims into the criminal justice network with special consideration for
the elderly. An extensive bibliography is provided.

244. Stiles, S. (1982). Meeting the need for crime analysis through
      volunteers. FBI Law Enforcement Bulletin, 51(11), 8–11.

This article focuses on the benefits of crime analysis for police
departments and then discusses how volunteers from the retired community
can perform many support functions in a crime analysis program. In the

crime analysis process, information is collected from incident reports
and other sources, examined for patterns and trends, and then
disseminated to officers. The final document facilitates patrol
deployment, provides investigative leads, directs crime prevention
activities, strengthens management decisions, and interagency
cooperation. A list of materials on crime analysis published by the
NRTA-AARP are provided.

245. Sunderland, G. (1980). Programming techniques. National
      Retired Teachers Association-AARP, Washington, D. C.

This document is written for the public relations police officer who
presents education and information programs for the community and, in
particular, for the implementation of programs for older audiences.
Included in this guide is a profile of aging which describes techniques
to enhance communication with the primary senses of vision and hearing.
Unique and creative ways to deliver information to an elderly audiences
is a major focus of this project.

246. Sunderland, G. (1976). The older american - police problem
      or police asset? FBI Law Enforcement Bulletin, 45(8), 3-8.

The program described in this article is the Crime Prevention Program of
the National Retired Teachers Association and the American Association
of Retired Persons which was originally intended for use among elderly
persons but which was adapted to a law enforcement effort as well. The
purpose of the article is to dispel myths of aging such as senility and
decreased mental abilities. Five situations in which the law
enforcement officer may have contact with an elderly person during the
performance of his duties are identified and described.

247. Sunderland, G., Cox, M. E., & Stiles, S. R. (1980). Law
      enforcement and older persons. National Retired Teachers
      Association - AARP, Washington, D. C.

This text provides a comprehensive training curriculum on law
enforcement and older persons. Topics focus on issues related to police
contact with older persons. Major topics include aging, victimization,
communication techniques, and volunteers in law enforcement. The text's
concluding section describes ten model resource program types and seven
actual cases of law enforcement programs involving older persons as
volunteers. Tables, charts, sample report forms, and references lists
are provided in this 380 page text.

248. Sunderland, G., Cox, M. E., & Stiles, S. R. (1980). Law
      enforcement and older persons - instructors guide. National
      Retired Teachers Association - AARP, Washington, D. C.

This instructor's guide is a comprehensive training curriculum designed
to improve local law enforcement officials' skills in working with
elderly to prevent crime against the elderly. The guide is divided into
16 lesson plans grouped into 4 separate modules. The guide is designed
to allow instructors the option of developing courses ranging from 2 to
40 hours in length. For each lesson, training objectives, lesson plans,
supporting visual aids, a discussion of major principles, key terms and
concepts, discussion questions, an examination with an answer key, and

student exercises are included. The four modules include: topics
related to general aging, victimization of the elderly, techniques for
dealing with older victims, and the establishment of an older volunteer
program within a law enforcement setting. Visual aids are provided.

249. Van Buren, D. P. (1976). Public housing security and the
      elderly: practice versus theory. In J. Goldsmith and S. S.
      Goldsmith (Eds.), Crime and the Elderly. Lexington,
      Massachusetts: D. C. Heath and Company.

The model of "defensible space" is advocated as a means of securing the
elderly in public housing. This is achieved through age-segregated
housing. In contrast, it is stated that residents in buildings which
employ uniformed security guards have an increased level of fear.
Defensible space uses informal social control to police their own
building. The lobby is the social center of activity, and few strangers
enter without being questioned. Age-segregated housing is proactive in
nature, not reactive, toward the crime problem. Formally structured
patrol activity seems to raise the level of fear instead of reducing it.

250. _____. (1978). Victim assistance for older adults program –
      model project. Northside Community Mental Health Center,
      Tampa, Florida.

This victim assistance program was developed to serve those 55 years of
age or older who have been the victim of a rape, robbery, assault,
burglary, larceny, or motor vehicle theft committed in Hillsborough
County. Victim information is received by the program from police
reports, referrals from other agencies, and from the victims themselves.
Response to the program from law enforcement authorities and from the
community has been most favorable. Program evaluations and staff
training are also briefly described. Case studies are included, and
data collection forms and references are provided.

251. Waddell, F. E. (1975). Consumer research and programs for the
      elderly – the forgotten dimension. Journal of Consumer
      Affairs, 9(2), 164–175.

The study summarizes existing knowledge of consumer problems,
exploitation, and needs of older people. While comprehensive in nature,
it reveals the lack of reliable data and research coming from
traditional consumer education programs important in the reduction of
fraudlent activities against the elderly. Several pilot programs are
introduced. Relevant references focusing on consumer research are
included.

252. Waddell, F. E., Garman, E. T., Harris, R. D., Hughston, G. A.,
      & Harrison, B. C. (1976). Consumer frauds and deceptions: a
      learning module. United States Office of Education,
      Washington, D. C.

The handbook is designed as a training manual for workshop leaders and
consumer education specialists in developing preventive crime programs
for the elderly. The training handbook includes modules composed of
reproducible user guide sections and media presentation consisting of
slide packets and cassette tapes. Types of frauds and deceptions

covered include land sale frauds, medical quackery, door to door sales
deceptions, pyramid promotions, mail order fraud, dance lesson and
health spa schemes, and hearing aid deceptions. The names and addresses
of Federal, State, and private agencies providing consumer problem
information are given.

253. Willis, R. L., & Miller, M. (1976). Senior citizen crime
      prevention program. Police Chief, 43, 16-17.

This article examines law enforcement in Cottage Grove, Oregon utilizing
the senior citizen population. Twenty-two percent of the population is
composed of people over sixty-five years of age, most of whom are on
fixed incomes. The traditional police role within Cottage Grove has
neglected to provide the elderly population with viable opportunities to
participate in the law enforcement initiative. With the advent of the
volunteer crime prevention designed by the police department, community
awareness and pride in the activities of senior volunteers has lowered
the crime rate in Cottage Grove, as well as raise the public
consciousness about crime.

254. Wolf, R. (1977). Senior citizen survey - an aid to designing
      prevention programs. Police Chief, 44(2), 27-29.

Results are provided of a 1976 Omaha Police Department survey on senior
center victimization, fears about crime, crime prevention habits, and
how crime affected their mobility. The 561 respondents were also given
an opportunity to suggest what type of crime prevention programs they
would be most interested in. Two separate groups of senior citizen made
up the survey: residents of city-operated senior citizen high-rise
apartments, and those living in private residences. Degree of
victimization is discussed in the findings. Burglary was the most
frequently committed crime, followed by larceny, robbery, and purse
snatching. Intervention strategies are also discussed.

255. Yagerlener, W. G. (1980). Crime prevention project. Walter
      P. Reuther Senior Centers, Detroit, MI.

This document describes the accomplishments of the Walter P. Reuther
Centers Crime Prevention Project in Detroit, Michigan, from November,
1978 to December, 1980. The initial purpose of the project was to
mobilize older persons and others in the community to become involved in
crime prevention activities in their neighborhoods, and to reduce crime
and the fear of crime among Detroit senior citizens. Various activities
to reduce the victimization of the elderly are described. The results
of surveys conducted at the start and at the conclusion of the project
indicate that the elderly participating in the project experienced a
reduction in victimization as well as a reduction in fear of crime. A
resource kit for other community organizations interested in developing
crimed prevention programs is included.

256. Yarmey, A. D., & Kent J. (1980). Eyewitness Identification by
      elderly and young adults. Law and Human Behavior, 4(4),
      359-371.

The accuracy of the elderly relative to young adults as witnesses to a
simulated crime was tested with measurements of verbal recall and facial

recognition. Twenty subjects each of groups of elderly men, elderly
women, young males, and young females observed a simulated assault and
theft of a wallet by a male assailant on a male victim. Young
subject-witnesses were significantly superior to the elderly in verbal
recall of details of the criminal episode. However, no reliable
differences were found between the two age categories in recognition of
the assailant or the victim. Women were superior to men and young
people were superior to the elderly in identifying the bystander. A
total of 21 references are provided.

257.   Younger, J. (1976). The California experience in crime
        prevention programs with senior citizens. In J. Goldsmith
        and S. S. Goldsmith (Eds.), Crime and the Elderly. Lexington,
        Massachusetts: D. C. Heath and Company.

The results of crime prevention programs for the elderly in California
are discussed at length. A profile of California's elderly is provided;
i.e., age, sex, health, geographic concentration, etc. Statistics and
brief generalizations of efforts for the elderly concerning crimes of
force, bunco and con games, medical quackery, and consumer fraud are
included as well. New methods of training aging agency personnel in
crime prevention are presented, as well as a list of federal, state,
local, and private organizations that are assisting in educating the
elderly in crime prevention.

258.   Younger, E. (1976). The California experience: prevention of
        criminal victimization of the elderly. The Police Chief,
        43(2), 28-32.

Describes the various ways the California elderly are vulnerable to
certain crimes. Provides reasons for the special vulnerability of the
elderly resulting from financial deprivation, physical deterioration,
inadequate housing, being isolated and lonely, and having a limited
access to transportation. A model is presented demonstrating how state,
local, federal, and private organizations have mobilized available
community resources in combating the criminal victimization of the
elderly in California.

II THE ELDERLY AS CRIMINALS

6 OLD AGE AND CRIME

259. Aday, R. H. (1984). Old Criminals. In E. Palmore (Ed.) <u>Handbook on the Aged in the United States.</u> Westport, Conn.: Greenwood Press.

A complete overview of crime in old age, including the statistical incidences of same, the demographic characteristics of elderly prisoners, and the types of crimes committed. Research on explanations of crime in old age points to poverty, alcohol abuse, loss of job and status, boredom after retirement, and long-time animosities as determinants of elderly crime. Prisoners' adjustment to prison life, their participation in activities and special programs pertinent to them are discussed. The various shortcomings of prior research on this subject and suggestions for more adequate research in the future are included. References are appended.

260. Alston, L. T. (1986). Older Deviants. In L. T. Alston (Ed.), <u>Crime and Older Americans.</u> Springfield, Illinois: Charles C. Thomas, Publisher.

A comprehensive overview of the older deviant is presented. Discussion is focused on serious crime such as violence as well as specific property offenses. General characteristics of the older offender are outlined. Deviant subgroups which commit crimes against public order and decency are also included. The relationship between age and criminal careers provides an important theoretical explanation for why certain crimes continue to decline in old age. Significant problems associated with aging which often leads to deviant behavior in old age are also addressed. An extensive bibliography is provided.

261. Boland, B. & Wilson, J. Q. (1978). Age, crime, and punishment. <u>Public Interest,</u> 51, 22-34.

This essay is mostly a theoretical working-paper. Its original intent was to address the issue of juvenile crime. However, some implications for elderly offenders are hidden within the article. The main focus of this article is a debate concerning the two-track approach court system; one for juveniles, one for adults. The authors critique the two-track system, pointing out the disadvantages. Their conclusions are: (1) some

significant punishment should befall all offenders; and (2) there should
not be two independent tracks, based on age, for serious repeat
offenders. The relevance of this article to the elderly concerns the
demand by some gerontologists to establish an independent court system
for the elderly, similar to the juvenile court.

262. Burnett, C. & Ortega, S. T. (1984). Elderly offenders: a
      descriptive analysis. In W. Wilbanks & P. K. Kim (Eds.),
      Elderly Criminals. New York: University Press.

This research examines the issue of a proposed geriatric crime wave by
examining in detail crime by various age groups over time. Data for
this study came from the arrest statistics of two midwestern communities
between the years of 1962 and 1967, and 1972 and 1980. Analysis is
limited to those arrests involving individuals 50 years of age and
older. Contrary to the crime wave hypothesis, the data demonstrates a
decline in arrest rates of persons age 50 and above. No relationship is
found between general economic hardship and arrest rates for property
crime or "personal disorganization misdemeanors." Much of the decline
in arrest rates is related to community alternatives to arrests for
alcohol-related offenses. Elaborate tables and graphs illustrate the
findings.

263. Cohen, F. (1985). Old age as a criminal defense. Criminal
      Law Bulletin, 21(1), 5-36.

The article describes and analyzes the characteristics of old age that
are relevant to the legal question of criminal responsibility and the
possible approaches to old age as a defense. Discussion focuses on the
following issues: aggravated culpability, diminished responsibility,
incapacity, no responsibility, age neutrality, and creation of a special
court for the elderly. The author then provides an analysis and
arguments for avoiding the acceptance of old age as a new defense.
Special attention is given to policy alternatives.

264. Cullen, F. T., Wozniak, J. F., & Frank, J. (1985). The rise
      of the elderly offender: will a "new" criminal be invented?
      Crime and Social Justice, 23, 151-165.

The general purpose of this article was to establish the basic pattern
of elderly crime and to determine if this pattern has increased over a
15 year period (1967-1982). The analysis is based on data from the FBI
Uniform Crime Reports including offenses measured as serious crime in
the FBI Crime Index. The authors utilize a variety of tables to
illustrate the point that elderly crime has not fluctuated all that much
over this particular time period. Conclusions are drawn as to why the
elderly offender has received so much attention without any significant
increase in criminal activity. While the authors conclude that the
elderly represent a potential problem, so significant trends have
emerged. Other social policy issues are also presented. Over ninety
references are provided.

265. Cutshall, C. R., & Adams, K. (1983). Responding to older
      offenders: age selectivity in the processing of shoplifters.
      Criminal Justice Review, 8(2), 1-8.

This article examines the effect of the offender's age upon private and public responses to shoplifting offenses at a number of key decision points in the criminal justice system. Using crosstabular analysis with simple elaboration techniques, the authors examine the decision to dismiss or prosecute charged shoplifting offenses against a trichotomous age classification. The findings demonstrate empirically that prosecutors selectively enforce legal norms against shoplifting, and that offender's age is a consideration in such decisions. The implications of these findings for the purpose of public policy and program development, and common perceptions about the criminality of older citizens are highlighted.

266. Duffee, E. D. (1984). A research agenda concerning crime by
      the elderly. In E. S. Newman, D. J. Newman, M. S. Gewirtz,
      (Eds.), Elderly Criminals. Cambridge, MA: Oelgeschlager, Gunn
      & Hain, Publishers, Inc.

This chapter addresses the need for research agendas to provide structure to the progress of inquiry into elderly crime. The author stresses the need to examine some of the larger factors dominant in American society rather than focusing on specific elderly deviants. The chapter raises some specific researchable questions about the incidence and causes of crime among the elderly as well as factors that enter into arrest and prosecution decisions. Topics include: responses to elderly crime, incidence and cause, and processing the elderly offender. The author concludes the chapter by discussing the role of research in policy formulation and suggests that researchers in both fields, gerontology and criminal justice, cooperate with each other and with policymakers in undertaking mutual efforts in this new area.

267. Feinberg, G. (1984). White haired offenders: an emergent
      social problem. In W. Wilbanks & P. K. Kim, (Eds.), Elderly
      Criminals. New York: University Press.

This chapter seeks to determine the extent and nature of criminality among the elderly. Taking a problems approach, basic research questions are posed on the following issues: causes, consequences and control of elderly crime. Uniform Crime Report tables as published by the F.B.I. over a fifteen year period (1966–80) were reviewed. Several additional findings were reported in characterizing elderly offenders: the most typical elderly crimes, changes in types of elderly criminality over time, elderly criminality and proportion of elderly in the population, elderly arrests and income, gender and elderly arrests and geographic distribution of elderly arrests. Extensive references are provided.

268. Greenberg, D. F. (1985). Age, crime, and social explanation.
      American Journal of Sociology, 91(1), 1–21.

This article examines closely the relationship between age and crime. In providing a causal analysis of crime, the issues associated with longitudinal versus cross-sectional research are addressed. In reviewing the crime rates for various age cohorts, it was found that rates for larceny and aggravated assault peaked rapidly in the early ages; however, in the postpeak years they remain constant to about age 60. The decline in the older years resulted most likely from declining strength. The author stresses the importance of utilizing longitudinal

or age-cohort data rather than cross-sectional data.   Extensive
references are provided.

269.   Malinchak, A. A.   (1980).   Crime and Gerontology.   New Jersey:
       Prentice-Hall, Inc.

This book discusses the elderly and their relationship to all aspects of
the criminal justice system.   The elderly as victims, as criminals, and
as volunteers in the system after retirement, are all areas of
discussion.   Disengagement and activity theory are used to speculatively
explain why the elderly engage in criminal behavior.   The author
concludes by recommending new programs and reforms of existing programs
that deal with the elderly and crime.   Lists are given of publications
concerning the elderly, organizations with information on the elderly,
and the state and regional agencies on aging.

270.   Malinchak, A. A.   (1978).   Embarrassing problem of elderly
       criminals.   Unpublished paper.   Florida State University
       School of Criminology, Tallahassee, FL.

This article attempts to provide a theoretical analysis and explanation
for the causes of crime committed by the elderly.   Disengagement and
activities are applied to the deviant behavior found among elderly
criminals.   It is suggested that basic reasons for the increase in crime
among the elderly (i.e., shoplifting and other misdemeanor crimes) are
the elderly's dependence on society and loss of functional roles in
society.   These factors, according to the author, are related to their
low income.   It is suggested that society can prevent further elderly
criminalization by improving social security benefits, abolishing
mandatory retirement, and making an effort to eliminate poverty and
economic frustrations experienced by the elderly.

271.   Morgan, I. P.   (1982).   The age and crime: geriatric
       delinquency.   Unpublished Paper, presented at the Arkansas
       Sociological Association in Fayetteville, Arkansas.

This paper explores the increasing criminality of the aged by: providing
a collection of social, cultural, and psychological references on the
aged; by sharing impressions about the conclusions of such references
focusing on the first time offender; and by analyzing the trends of
arrest of the elderly for all arrestees, arrestees for index crimes and
arrestees for other crimes in Arkansas 1979 to 1981.   Descriptive
findings are presented.

272.   Newman, E. S. & Newman, D. J.   (1984).   Public policy
       implications of elderly crime.   In E. S. Newman, D. J. Newman,
       M. L. Gewirtz, (Eds.), Elderly Criminals.   Cambridge, MA:
       Oelgeschlager, Gunn & Hain, Publishers, Inc.

This chapter addresses those factors inherent in the establishment of
elderly crime as a policy related issue.   General awareness of elderly
crime by the public as well as the fate of the elderly in the criminal
justice system provided two major themes.   It is suggested that the
criminal justice should be sensitive to the special problems of older
persons at each stage of criminal processing.   For example, arrest,
pretrial release, pretrial diversion, alternative sentencing, probation,

and incarceration are outlined as areas calling for special attention.
A number of social issues which contribute to the elderly's
post-retirement problems are also included.

273. Newman, D. & Newman, E. S. (1982). Senior citizen crime.
      Justice Reporter, 2(5), 1-7.

The authors review the phenomenon of the elderly offender, the types of
crime they commit, and the need for the criminal justice system to
consider alternative crime control and punishment strategies. This
article focuses on homicide, sex and drug crimes, shoplifting, organized
crime, and assaults. It was concluded that a disproportionately high
number of elderly prison inmates are serving time for homicide, assault,
and serious sex crimes. Most researchers see the increasing elderly
crime rate as representing a shift in age demography than a direct
increase in the percentage of elderly involved in crime. No statistical
tables are presented, but a useful profile of the elderly offender is
included.

274. Newman, E. S., Newman, D. J. & Gewirtz, M. L. (1984).
      Elderly Criminals. Massachusetts: Oelgeschlager, Gunn &
      Hain Publishers, Inc.

This book examines the issue of elderly crime, and raises questions as
to how appropriately the current criminal justice system deals with the
elderly offender. The nationwide extent of elderly crime, the types of
offenses committed by older criminals, and the criminal justice system
are all discussed. Although no elderly crime wave is indicated by
statistics, these authors feel the total number of crimes committed by
the elderly will increase as the numbers of elderly increase in the
population. Alternative methods of dealing with this problem are
presented, and questions raised as to future research.

275. Rowe, A. R. (1983). Sanctions and the aged woman.
      Perceptual and Motor Skills, 56, 427-430.

This study concerns how women perceive and judge an aged female
offender. Fifty randomly selected women were asked to hypothetically
sentence an aged female on four crimes: (1) "taking something that did
not belong to her worth about $50;" (2) "physically harming somebody on
purpose;" (3) "gambling illegally;" and (4) "cheating on income tax."
Results were that when immorality was not an issue, women 65 years and
older were virtually exempt from punishment. When found guilty of a
crime concerning morality, i.e., gambling, they were sentenced almost as
severely as other women. One table. References.

276. Shichor, D. (1985). Male-female differences in elderly
      arrests: an exploratory analysis. Justice Quarterly, 2(3),
      399-414.

Utilizing arrest statistics, this research compares the crime patterns
of elderly males and females. The findings reveal that there are more
differences in arrest between elderly males and females than between
males and females in the general population. Comprehensive arrest
patterns based on age and sex are presented. Statistical tables are
appropriately utilized. The issue of differential handling of females

and the elderly by law enforcement agencies could not be dealt with
sufficiently using these statistics.

277.   Shichor, D., & Solomon K. (1978). Note: criminal behavior
        among the elderly. The Gerontologist, 18, 213-218.

This article gives a brief overview of the many aspects of elderly
offenders. Basically, elderly offenders receive more lenient treatment
by criminal justice agencies. The elderly are called a relatively
powerless group at present. However, as the number of elderly persons
continue to grow, political power and civic status will increase. This
is predicted to bring about a harsher treatment of elderly offenders in
the future, thus attributing more responsibility for their actions.
Problems that will confront criminal justice agencies are discussed as
well.

278.   Shichor, D. (1984). The extent and nature of lawbreaking by the
        elderly: a review of arrest statistics. In E. S. Newman, D. J.
        Newman, & M. L. Gewirtz, (Eds.), Elderly Criminals. Cambridge,
        MA: Oelgeschlager, Gunn & Hain, Publishers, Inc.

This chapter is designed to review and analyze the extent and nature of
involvement in lawbreaking behavior by the elderly. Analysis is based
on the arrest statistics of the FBI's Uniform Crime Reports at five-year
intervals between 1964 and 1979. Comparisons are made between the
55-and-over age group and the general population. Increase in arrest of
the elderly was moderate for the fifteen-year period. Policy notations
are made concerning the need for increased research. Numerous tables
are provided to illustrate arrest data.

279.   Silverman, M., Smith, L. G., Nelson, C., & Dembo, R. (1984).
        The perception of the elderly criminal when compared to adult
        and juvenile offenders. Journal of Applied Gerontology, 3,
        97-104.

The purpose of this study was to ascertain how elderly criminals were
perceived compared to adult or juvenile criminals. Also, variations in
punishments were considered as well. Respondents were divided into 3
groups of elderly, college students, and police officers. A
questionnaire was then administered describing a crime and a list of
attributes for six conditions in which age and sex varied. Conclusions
drawn from the study are that the elderly are perceived more positively
than adults or juveniles and a more lenient sentence was granted for the
elderly by the respondents. References.

280.   Smith, E. D., and Hed A. (1979). Effects of
        offenders' age and attractiveness on sentencing by mock
        juries. Psychological Reports, 44, 691-694.

In this study, mock juries were assembled and shown pictures of both
attractive and unattractive women, young and old alike. Case reports
were attached to each picture describing a swindle or a burglary. The
juries, composed of three females each, were asked to pass sentence
between 1 and 10 years for each case. Older individuals were sentenced
more severely than younger ones. For burglary, attractive individuals
received less severe sentences than the unattractive individuals. When

the swindle condition was described, attractiveness had no bearing on
the sentencing decision.

281.   Steffensmeier, D. J. (1987). The invention of the "new" senior
        citizen criminal. Research On Aging, 9(2), 281-311.

Based on Uniform Crime Reports' arrest statistics for the years of
1964-1984, this article examines the arrest rates for the past twenty
years for these 65 years of age and over. Three major questions are
addressed: (1) whether the rate of increase in elderly crime is greater
than the increase in the elderly population of the United States during
1964-1984, (2) whether the rate of increase is greater than the increase
for other age groups, and (3) whether within the elderly arrest
population there has been a change in the profile of the elderly
offender toward involvement in more serious crime. Trends in elderly
rates by type of crime are illustrated in numerous tables. An extensive
bibliography is included.

282.   Sunderland, G.   (1982). Geriatric crime wave: the great
        debate. Police Chief, 49(10), 40, 42, 44.

The author dispells the myth that there is an epidemic of elderly
offenders committing crimes. These myths are perpetuated by the media.
In reality, the elderly are primarily arrested for DUI and public drunk.
Virginia, California, Florida, and Colorado arrest statistics reaffirm
that no epidemic exists. It is shown how actual numbers can be
manipulated into percentages, depicting a jump in elderly crime.   Small
numbers are often exaggerated into huge percentages. Two tables
containing UCR data (1981) are included.

283.   Wilbanks, W. (1985).   Are elderly felons treated more
        leniently by the criminal justice system? A paper presented at
        the Third National Conference on Elderly Offenders, Kansas City,
        Missouri.

Utilizing data from the California Offender Based Transaction System
(OBTS), 1562 cases of elderly offenders were compared to 160,413 cases
of offenders ages 20-59, to see if the elderly are treated more
leniently. It was found that the elderly are treated more harshly at
conviction and more leniently at sentencing. Leniency was not found for
all offenses. However, the appearance of leniency is due to the variety
of offenses for which the elderly are convicted. Sex and race were
found to be better predictors of treatment by the criminal justice
system.

284.   Wilbanks, W. & Kim, P. K. (1984).   Elderly Criminals.
        New York: University Press.

This book is a collection of papers, or articles, most of which were
presented at a conference on the elderly offender. Two of the articles
disprove the much-tented media claim that there is a geriatric crime
wave. Other articles discuss the diversity of characteristics within
the elderly criminal population, the patterns of elderly crime in three
types of communities, the similarity of elderly violent offenders to
young violent offenders, and characteristics of the elderly shoplifter.
One study found that elderly criminals are labelled with less negative

attributes than younger offenders, although they are not necessarily treated more leniently. The last article discusses the use of diversion programs with the elderly and the success of one such program.

7 ELDERLY CRIME PATTERNS

285. Brown, B. B., & Chiang, C. (1983). Drug and alcohol abuse among the elderly: is being alone the key? <u>International Journal of Aging and Human Development,</u> 18(1), 1-12.

Using data from interviews with older clients over the age of 55, a profile of drug and alcohol abusers is provided. Relying on a special sample (N=21 in drug treatment facilities; 30 not in treatment; and 155 nonabusers) characteristics of social background and support are compared. Substance abuse appeared more prevalent among single and divorced elderly and among residents who lived alone. The presence or absence of living companions was more influential than relationships with nearby social supports. Implications for health and social service programs, as well as for further research, are discussed.

286. Curran, D. (1984). Characteristics of the elderly shoplifter and the effect of sanctions on recidivism. In W. Wilbanks & P. K. Kim (Eds.), <u>Elderly Criminals.</u> New York: University Press.

A study examines the characteristics of elderly shoplifters from Palm Beach County, Florida based on records for three samples: all 176 elderly shoplifters arrested by the county sheriff's office in 1981, all 234 elderly shoplifters completing a pretrial diversion program in 1980, and all 83 elderly shoplifters apprehended in a retail establishment in the county in 1977-81. Results indicate that elderly shoplifters are average citizens caught stealing trivial items. They are sanctioned like other shoplifters, with disposition based on prior arrest and value of the item stolen. Age is not a significant predictor of case disposition. Only 1% of the sample had a record of a subsequent arrest for shoplifting or any other offense. While the elderly shoplifters do not appear to be a major problem for the criminal justice system, this chapter does provide an excellent profile.

287. Feinberg, G. (1984). Profile of the elderly shoplifter. In E. S. Newman, D. J. Newman, & M. L. Gewirtz (Eds.). <u>Elderly Criminals.</u> Cambridge, MA: Oelgeschlager, Gunn & Hain, Publishers, Inc.

Based on a sample of 191 elderly shoplifter cases, this chapter provides
a most descriptive profile of the elderly shoplifter. Numerous elderly
shoplifting myths as well as other general characteristics are
presented. Baseline crime data and a theoretical comparison of elderly
and juvenile delinquents suggest implications for social policy. The
chapter suggests the necessity to understand certain role losses, role
disengagement as well as role acquisition experienced by the elderly.
It is suggested that the transition into old age provide enough stress
to create deviance. The Broward Senior Intervention and Education
Program designed specifically to rehabilitate the elderly shoplifter is
briefly described.

288. Fyfe, J. F. (1984). Police dilemmas in processing elderly
      offenders. In E. S. Newman, D. J. Newman & M. L. Gewirtz,
      (Eds.), Elderly Criminals. Cambridge, MA: Oelgeschlager, Gunn
      & Hain, Publishers, Inc.

The author discusses the police decision of whether to take elderly
offenders into custody and, if so, the amount of force that is
necessary. Shoplifting and family violence are used as case
illustrations. Police dilemmas in processing elderly offenders are
addressed. It is concluded that most police are not adequately trained
in dealing with elderly offenders, and jails often can be traumatic for
the elderly. It is suggested that police need to learn to deal
effectively with elderly offenders who can sometimes be senile and
aggressive. Alternate ways the police have developed for handling older
offenders are outlined.

289. Golden, D. (1984). Elderly offenders in jail. In E. S. Newman,
      D.J. Newman, & M. L. Gewirtz (Eds), Elderly Criminals.
      Cambridge, Mass: Oelgeschlager, Gunn & Hain, Publishers, Inc.

This chapter describes the role that jails play in the incarceration of
offenders. The special problem elderly offenders face in this
particular environment are addressed. Topics such as admission
procedures, medical screening and the physical structure of the jail
itself are discussed. The Albany jail in New York is described more
specifically. Case histories are utilized to provde a descriptive
profile for first-time offenders. Research and policy implications are
evident. Tables are provided.

290. Gross, D. & Capuzzi, D. (1981). The elderly alcoholic: the
      counselor's dilemma. Counselor Education and Supervision,
      20, 183-192.

This article examines the physiological, psychological, and sociological
factors associated with an elderly person becoming an alcoholic, from
the viewpoint of a professional counselor. As people grow older, they
may become susceptible and more vulnerable to increased economic,
health, and social problems. The aging alcoholic appears to be the
least visible among all sufferers of addictive problems. Surveys
indicate that little is being offered in current counselor education
programming to prepare the counselor to work with the elderly, and less
programming is available to deal with the elderly addictive individual.

291. Hiday, V. A. & Atkinson, M. P. (1984). The aged and the
      dangerousness criterion in involuntary civil commitment.

1(2), 195–205.

Utilizing data from official court records and observations in court hearings throughout the state of North Carolina, this study investigates the elderly against whom petitions are brought for involuntary civil commitment. In relation to their proportion in the population, the aged are only slightly more likely than younger persons to become respondents in commitment proceedings; but they are over three times more likely to remain involuntarily hospitalized and to be subjected to recommitment proceedings. In analyzing court testimony, the authors found that almost half of the old have no testimony alleging dangerous behavior. The alleged dangerous acts of the aged tend to be unintentional harm rather than assault. Suggestions for policy alternatives are provided.

292. Hucker, S. J. (1984). Psychiatric aspects of crime in old age. In E. S. Newman, D. J. Newman, & M. L. Gewirtz, (Eds.), Elderly Criminals. Cambridge, MA: Oelgeschlager, Gunn & Hain, Publishers, Inc.

This chapter summarizes two groups of incarcerated elderly offenders who were referred for psychiatric examination. The major focus of this research included individuals aged 60 years or older – 45 sex offenders and 16 violent offenders. In both cases these offenders were compared to a comparable sampes aged 30 or younger. This study concludes that while research samples are difficult to obtain, this research helps provide a clearer picture of the characteristics of cases likely to be interviewed at porenisic psychiatric facilities. Despite methodological problems, this study calls for a thorough psychiatric, neurological, and social work evaluation of elderly offenders.

293. Hucker, S. J. & Ben–Aron, M. H. (1984). Violent elderly offenders: a comparative study. In W. Wilbanks, & P. K. Kim, (Eds.), Elderly Criminals. New York: University Press.

This research provides a psychiatric perspective on violent elderly offenders referred by the courts to a clinic in Toronto. A total of 48 clinical files were reviewed by the authors. For comparative purposes, a group of individuals aged 30 years or younger were randomly matched with elderly violent patients charged with the same offense. While it is difficult to locate large elderly samples, similar differences for this study did emerge between violent offenders from the separate age categories. Comparative tables and a comprehensive statistical analysis are provided.

294. Jennison, M. K. (1984). The violent older offender: a research note. Federal Probation, 50(3), 60–65.

The article attempts to link the excessive use of alcohol to elderly criminal behavior. Utilizing 292 inmates in locally operated jails, over 80 variables were categorized into four broad categories: sociodemographic data; offender history and previous contact with the criminal justice system, employment history; and variables related to drinking behavior and alcohol consumption in the year before incarceration. Statistical correlations and regressions are provided. The study suggests a definite need for alcohol rehabilitation among elderly offenders as well as a need for widespread alcohol screening at the judicial level. Excellent reference source.

295. Keller, O. J, & Vedder, C. B. (1968). The crimes that old
      persons commit. The Gerontologist, 8(1), 43-50.

Utilizing the Uniform Crime Reports, this article provides a
descriptive analysis of elderly criminality. One of the initial studies
on the topic, the authors integrate the previous literature into their
findings. Special crimes such as sexual offenses, crimes of violence,
homicide and suicide, and fraud are fully discussed. Several tables are
used to display profiles of the elderly offenders.

296. Kratcoski, P. C. & Walker, D. B. (1986). Homicide among the
      elderly: analysis of victim/assailant relationships. Presented
      at the Academy of Criminal Justice Science Conference in Orlando,
      Florida.

This research provides a clear rationale for the study of the elderly
criminal. In particular, the paper cites the need for needed research
in the area of elderly homicide. An excellent summary of related
literature is presented. Drawing from the literature, eight hypotheses
are offered for testing. Based on a larger sample from Cuyahoga County
Ohio, for the years 1970-1983, 82 cases comprising elderly homicide
offenders were included. These cases (age 60 and over) were compared
with other homicide offenders grouped into age categories of 5-14 and
15-59. Descriptive findings are presented along with ten tables for
analysis purposes.

297. McIntosh, J. L. (1985). Suicide among the elderly: levels and
      trends. American Journal of Orthopsychiatry, 55(2), 288-293.

The article reviews U.S. suicide rates which continues to be highest
among the elderly. In particular, the white, elderly male is singled
out. Suicide thus represents a major mental health problem for a
much-neglected age group. National levels and trends of suicide among
the aged are presented by sex and race for 1933-1978. Explanations of
these trends are considered, and information is provided on recognition
and prevention of geriatric suicide.

298. Meyers, A. (1984). Drinking, problem drinking, and
      alcohol-related crime among older people. In E. S. Newman,
      D. J. Newman, & M. L. Gewirtz, (Eds.), Elderly Criminals.
      Cambridge, MA: Oelgeschlager, Gunn & Hain, Publishers, Inc.

Utilizing national crime statistics, this chapter addresses some of the
more important research and policy questions associated with alcohol and
crime in old age. Although there are methodological limitations, the
author successfully develops a better informed agenda for social policy.
Prevailing theories associated with a excessive drinking and
alcohol-related law enforcement problems among the elderly are
presented. An extensive rationale for future research needs is an added
bonus. Topics such as longitudinal studies, police behavior and special
needs and circumstances of older drinkers and drivers are presented.
Tables are included.

299. Newman, D. J. (1984). Elderly offenders and American crime

patterns. In E. S. Newman, D. J. Newman, & M. L. Gewirtz,
(Eds.), <u>Elderly Criminals.</u> Cambridge, MA: Oelgeschlager, Gunn
& Hain, Publishers, Inc.

This chapter focuses on the extent of crimes by the elderly. Emphasis
is given to the involvement of elderly persons in all types of crime:
organized, white-collar, professional, and conventional street crime.
The ways that these crimes are defined and the role that age plays in
criminal activity is also discussed. This overview concludes that the
elderly play a more prominent role in major crime patterns than is
commonly believed. It is further concluded that the elderly may be the
most underarrested category of offenders except for the very young.
Challenges facing the criminal justice system are also addressed.

300. Richman, J. (1982). Homicidal and assaultive behavior in the
      elderly. In B. L. Danto (Ed.), <u>Human Side of Homicide.</u> New
      York, New York: Columbia University Press.

This chapter provides an analysis of cases involving homicide or
assaults by elderly persons. Theoretical explanations for homicidal or
violent acts among the elderly is addressed. Studies of violent
behavior by the elderly indicate that the victim is usually known to the
offender and that the behavior is associated with problems of aging,
illness, and the decline of coping abilities. It is concluded that
while the overall incidence of crime by the elderly is low, the relative
incidence of homicide and aggravated assault is high, and the percentage
of elderly arrested for such crimes has risen steadily. Suggestions for
more comprehensive studes are included.

301. Sapp, A. D. (1985). Arrests for major crimes: friends and
      patterns for elderly offenders. Unpublished paper. <u>Center
      for Criminal Justice Research,</u> Central Missouri State
      University.

This paper analyzes the trends and patterns of arrests of the elderly
for the major crimes reported in the Annual Uniform Crime Reports for
the years 1972 through 1981. A comprehensive and most descriptive
account of arrest for those over 55 is provided. While violent offenses
declined during their period, property offenses increased significantly
in the ten year study period. Several figures and tables are utilized
for illustration purposes. An extensive bibliography is included.

302. Shichor, D. (1984). Patterns of elderly lawbreaking in urban
      suburban and rural areas: what do arrest statistics tell us?
      In W. Wilbanks, & P. K. Kim (Eds.), <u>Elderly Criminals.</u>
      New York: University Press.

This research is an analysis of the arrest patterns of elderly offenders
55 years and older in the geographic areas: cities, suburbs, and rural
areas. The analysis focuses on the percent changes over time in elderly
arrests versus the general population across the three ecological
groups. Based on the <u>Uniform Crime Reports</u> for 1964, 1969, 1974, and
1979, the article presents several comprehensive findings with
accompanying tables. Extensive references.

303. Silverman, M., Smith, L. G., Nelson, C., and Kosberg, J.

(1984). The perception of the elderly criminal compared to
adult and juvenile offenders. In W. Wilbanks & P. K. Kim,
(Eds.), Elderly Criminals. New York: University Press.

This study utilizes an experimental design to address the question of
the extent to which the age variable affects the stigmatization that
normally occurs when an individual is labeled criminal. The subjects
considered were two groups of 34 respondents selected on the basis of
age. One group of subjects was over the age of 60 white the second
group consisted of college students with a mean age of 20. Utilizing
the attribution theory, the study was designed to evaluate the effects
of age as a mitigating factor in the assignment of stereotyped
perceptions to individuals accused of being involved in criminal
activities. Attributes are separately listed in table form.
Appropriate statistics and an extensive bibliography are included.

304. Stover, N. (1985). Aging Criminals. Beverly Hills,
      California: Sage Publications, Inc.

The text examines the problems of stigma management, interpersonal
relationships, and the array of criminal offenses for aging adults. The
source of data is personal interviews with 50 men, all of whom were
incarcerated at least once for ordinary property crimes. The interview
data are supplemeted by analysis of the subjects' correctional records.
The effect of multiple prison experiences on the aging criminal is
successfully illustrated and the inability of control theory to account
for repeated offenses is emphasized. The despairs, satisfactions, and
uncertainties of the aging criminal are discussed. Case studies and
illustrations are presented.

305. Wilbanks, W. (1984). The elderly offender: sex and race
      variations in frequency and pattern. In W. Wilbanks, & P. K.
      Kim, (Eds.), Elderly Criminals. New York: University Press.

This chapter examines the degree of homogeneity in the category of the
elderly offender. Data consisted of 3,477 misdemeanor charges and 791
felony charges for those 60 years of age and older as reported in 1982
in Dade County, Florida. Findings indicate that there is tremendous
variation in frequency of commission (measured by rates) and patterns of
offenses by sex, race, sex/race, and age. Age within the elderly
offender category is as good a predictor of felony rates as is sex.
Petty theft/shoplifting was the most frequent misdemeanor charge for the
elderly offender. Grand theft and possession and the role of narcotics
were the most frequent felony charges. Tables and references are
included.

306. Wilbanks, W. (1984). The elderly offender: placing the
      problem in perspective. In W. Wilbanks & P. K. Kim, (Eds.),
      Elderly Offender. New York: University Press.

This research compares the relative frequency of crimes by the elderly
to that of other age categories. Comparisons were made utilizing the
Uniform Crime Reports for the years 1970 and 1980. In this case, the
elderly were defined as all persons 60 years of age or older. While it
is concluded that crime by the elderly is not increasing faster than
that for other age groups, it does provide an excellent profile of the

elderly offender. In this profile, specific questions are answered
regarding increasing crime among the elderly (violence vs larceny, etc)
as future predictions of the crime rate as the population ages.
Extensive tables are included.

307. Wilbanks, W., & Murphy, D. D. (1984). The elderly homicide
      offender. In E. S. Newman, D. J. Newman & M. L. Gewirtz,
      (Eds.), Elderly Criminals. Cambridge, Mass: Oelgeschlager,
      Gunn & Hain, Publishers, Inc.

Utilizing a national data tape of homicides, this chapter presents eight
research hypotheses about elderly homicide offenders. The elderly
offender was defined as sixty years or older with the oldest elderly
homicide offender being ninety-three years old. A number of
correlations were concluded by such variables as: race of offender by
race of victim; elderly versus nonelderly; type of homicide, weapon
choice, etc. Statistical techniques and tables are provided. Measures
of association provided no general theory but major research questions
are proposed. Important implications for social policy are suggested by
the authors.

8 CAUSES OF CRIMINAL BEHAVIOR

308. Aday, R. H. (1981). The Aging Prisoner: A Comparative analysis of first and chronic offenders. Unpublished paper. Department of Sociology, Middle Tennessee State University.

An overview is given of previous research done on older prisoners and the differences between first time and repeat offenders. Upon looking at research conducted on determinants of crime in old age, the author concludes that poverty, alcohol abuse, loss of job and status, boredom after retirement, and long-time animosities are commonly responsible for old age crime. The author gathered data from elderly prisoners and found differences between first-timers and recidivists with regard to types of crime committed, marital status, vists from outsiders, ability to rely on someone for parole, and the degree of dependency on the institution.

309. Hirschi, T. & Gottfredson, M. (1984). Age and the explanation of crime. America Journal of Sociology, 89(3), 552-584.

Provides an in-depth discussion of the role that age plays as a predictor variable for expalaining criminal activity. A thorough review of the literature contributes to the discussion. The authors conclude that while age is frequently correlated with crime, it is not a very useful variable in predicting involvement in crime over the life cycle of offenders. Several graphs are used to present these findings. The general conclusion drawn is that longitudinal study is not required to study the causes of crime across the life cycle. Implications for future research as well as various policy issues are appropriately addressed. Excellent reference source.

310. Ilse, J. A. (1985). Growing old and going straight: examining the role of age in criminal career termination. Unpublished Dissertation. Portland State University.

This study was designed to investigate mid-life problems from crime as a specific function of general mid-life change. The adandoment of a criminal career at mid-life is seen as a significant occupational and lifestyle change. Major topics reviewed which in conjunction with transitional processes include: work and social relationships, and psychological well-being. Structured interviews were conducted with a group of former career criminals and a group of currently imprisoned middle-aged career offenders. Career offenders were compared with middle age general population men, and former career offenders were compared with imprisoned career offenders. Limitations of the research design and the sampling methods are also discussed.

311. Kart, G. S. (1981). In the matter of Earle Spring: some thoughts on one court's approach to senility. The Gerontologist, 21, 417-423.

This article is a detailed case study of how three Massachusetts courts (Probate, Appeals, and Supreme Court) found that senility was just cause to terminate medical treatment. Mr. Spring, a senile patient, suffered from chronic kidney failure. Included in the article is a detailed look at Mr. Spring's health history, the court's misuse of the terms "senility" and "organic brain syndrome," and other aspects of the court's approach that is inconsistent with current gerontological knowledge. Excellent bibliography. Court case citations.

312. Kercher, K. (1987). The causes and correlates of crime committed by the elderly. Research on Aging, 9(2), 256-280.

The article examines the variables that tend to influence the illegal behavior of older persons. The research attempts to answer the question: are the causes and correlates of crime the same for older as for younger age groups? While an attempt is made to assess the empirical evidence concerning the causes and correlates of crime by the elderly, for the most part, it is done in a very different way. The major variables discussed include: age, race, and sex, marital status, religious commitment, residential mobility, prior criminal behavior, socioeconomic status, anomie, criminal associates, attachment to others, criminal beliefs and deterrence factors. A most thorough synthesis of the literature. A total of 109 references are appended.

313. McCreary, C. P., & Mensh, I. N. (1977). Personality differences associated with age in law offenders. Journal of Gerontology, 32, 164-167.

This study reports the results of 362 MMPI profiles of male law offenders, divided into six large age groups. The purpose of the study was to determine patterns of personality disturbance in older vs. younger offenders. Older offenders were found to have more neurotic tendencies and less psychotic or anti-social tendencies than younger offenders. This reaffirms the claim that the problems of the elderly (i.e., drunkeness and vagrancy) should be handled in "noncriminal" settings, and should not be jailed or fined. Two tables. References.

314. Miller, L. (1979). Toward a classification of aging behaviors. The Gerontologist, 19, 283-290.

This is a very interesting article that attempts to classify aging behaviors, from legitimate behaviors to deviant behaviors. The main purpose of the article is to illustrate how behaviors in adulthood, such as self-management, self-regulation, productivity, purposefulness, and productive work, slowly give way to illegitimate behaviors associated

with old age. Miller has constructed an index that lists 18
illegitimate, conditionally legitimate, and unconditionally legitimate
behaviors related to self care, task behaviors, and relationship
behavior. References.

315.   Rodstein, M. (1975). Crime and the aged: the criminals.
       Journal of the American Medical Association, 234, 639.

This article is a brief synopsis of the aged as perpetrators of crime
rather than as victims. Special discussion is provided regarding the
incidence of crime among the elderly and the general reactions of the
criminal justice system. Most important, however, is the author's
attempt to explain the causes for the etiology of crime appearing for
the first time late in life. These findings were based on a series of
interviews with 24 highly qualified judges, jurists, lawyers, district
attorneys, probation officers, psychiatrists, and welfare workers who
have had experience with approximately 5,000 reported offenses by
indivduals 60 years and older.

9 AGING PRISONERS

316. Aday, R. H. (1976). <u>Institutional dependency: a theory of aging in prison.</u> Unpublished dissertation, Oklahoma State University.

In an attempt to develop a tentative model of aging in prison, two separate samples of older prisoners are included. One sample was composed of 40 older prisoners from a medium security facility and another sample of 55 older prisoners from a maximum security institution. While the average age of the sample was 62, ages ranged from 55 to 82 years. Structured questionnaires are utilized focusing on demographic data, reference groups, institutional dependency, life satisfaction, social activities, and the prisoners' correctional history. Quantitative and qualitative findings are presented in descriptive and tabular form. It is found that the variables of marital status, length of imprisonment, and differences in criminal classification tend to support the model of institutional dependency. The appendix contains the survey instruments, the institutional dependency index, and an extensive bibliography.

317. Aday, R. H. & Webster, E. L. (1979). Aging in prison: the development of a preliminary model. <u>Offender Rehabilitation,</u> 3(3), 271-282.

An exploratory attempt to establish a more systematic model of aging in prison is made in this study. The prison population included 94 older male inmates at two separate prisons. The concept of institutional dependence of older prisoners provides the major focus for this study. Demographic data is provided for the subjects. The average age of the population was 61 years, and 29 percent of the older prisoners were married. Structured interviews were utilized to obtain information on life satisfaction, institutional adjustment, health problems, prison activities, and criminal characteristics. Institutional dependency was found to be linked to marital status, length of imprisonment, and age at first imprisonment. Chronic offenders were found to exhibit more institutional dependency than those who committed their first offense at a later age. Statistical tables, questionnaire items and extensive references are provided.

318.   Chaneles, S. (1987). Growing old behind bars. Psychology
        Today, October, 46-51.

This brief article presents insightful accounts of the special needs and
problems of aging prisoners. Based on personal interviews with several
elderly prisoners, the author provides information on their daily lifes
and general means of coping with the prison system as a whole. Such
topics as social security, health care needs, types of crimes committed,
and general policy issues are discussed. Comparisons are made between
various state and federal programs which impact on the elderly offender.

319.   Cox, J. (1982).   Self-perceptions of health and aging of older
        females in prison: an exploraory age group case study. Unpub-
        lished Dissertation, Southern Illinois University.

This study conducted in a state prison for women explored the
demographic characteristics, self-perceived health status, and the
perceptions of aging of three prisoner age groups: young 17-29; mid-age
30-39; and 40 and over. Based on open-ended interviews, a comprehensive
individual portrait was established. The findings indicated that
generally older women registered a high number of physical complaints,
but fewer emotional and spiritual problems. Older women also expressed
much more positive views of aging than did younger women. The author
suggested that further studies carefully analyze food services, exercise
opportunities and general health attitudes within the prison
environment. Tabular information, interview schedule, and references
are appended.

320.   Flanagan, T. J. (1981). Dealing with long-term confinement:
        adaptive strategies and perspectives among long-term prisoners.
        Criminal Justice and Behavior, 8(2), 204-222.

This study discusses the consequences of aging in prison. Reviewing
recent research, outcomes of long-term confinement such as physical
condition, personality deterioration, psychopathological effects, and
self esteem are addressed. Data is reported on 59 inmates who had
served at least five years of continuous confinement. A preliminary
model of aging in prison is presented. Utilizing a developmental
approach, experiences in the prison environment across time which
impacts on future perspectives such as behavioral and attitudinal
ramifications are discussed.

321.   Flanagan, T.J. (1982). Lifers and long-termers: doing big time.
        In R. Johnson & H. Toch (Eds.), The Pains of Imprisonment.
        Berverly Hills, California: Sage Publications.

This chapter focuses on the special problems and stresses faced by
offenders serving long prison sentences, particularly those serving life
terms. Distinctions are made between the general pains of imprisonment
and the consequences of being a long-term prisoner. Various coping and
adaptive strategies are presented. Topics such as philosophy of
"minimum expectations," "here and now," and "campaigning," are
addressed. While not aimed exclusively at the aging prisoner, this
article provides useful insights into the process of growing old in
prison. References are provided.

322. French, L. (1979). Prison sexualization: inmate adaptations to
      psycho-sexual stress. Corrective and Social Psychiatry and
      Journal of Behavior Technology Methods and Therapy, 25(2),
      64-69.

Various ways in which prisoners adapt to the psychosexual stress of
prison life are presented. Based on studies of sex and stress in the
prison systems of three states, the process of prisonization,
particularly the introduction of inmates into a sexually perverse
environment, is described. Distinctions are made between younger
inmates and older inmates who may be serving life sentences. Sexual
lifestyles and options available in the prison environment are assessed.
Various means of coping with the stressors of prison life are addressed.
References are included.

323. Gillespie, M. W. & Galliher, J. F. (1972). Age, anomie and the
      inmate's definition of aging in prison: an exploratory study.
      In D. P. Kent, R. Kastenbaum and S. Sherwood (Eds.), Research
      Planning and Action for the Elderly, New York: Behavioral
      Publications, Inc.

Comparisons are made between the inmate's definition of aging in prison
and three correlations of anomie. A major focus of the article centers
around the definitions of growing old in prison and whether it is a
preserving experience or an aging experience due to the hostile
environment. An important definition of aging in prisons seems to
depend, not on the length of sentence remaining, but the age of the
offender. The older the offender the more pessimistic their view of the
prison experience. In order to draw specific conclusions regarding
anomie, the authors suggest that additional research is necessary.
Several tables help to describe the statistical data. References are
appended.

324. Goetting, A. (1985). Racism, sexism, and ageism in the prison
      community. Federal Probation, 49(1), 10-22.

The article compares the differences between prison society and the
larger free community in this country in terms of minority relations.
Blacks, women and the elderly are examined as specific subjects of
discrimination by means of both formal and informal prison practices.
Due to their distinct differences, each group is analyzed separately.
The comparison of prison practices where male and female prisoners are
concerned is particularly comprehensive. Differentials between men and
women inmates are demonstrated for: remoteness, heterogeneity,
institutional services, physical environment, recreational facilities,
institutional staff, educational and vocational programs and industrial
programs. Attitudes toward the elderly inmate are discussed, and the
lack of prison programs for the aging inmate is brought to the
forefront. Ninety references are included.

325. Goetting, A. (1984). The elderly in prison: a profile.
      Criminal Justice Review, 9(2), 14-24.

From a 1979 nationwide self-report survey of 11,397 inmates in state
penal institutions, 248 of them aged 55 or older, a profile of elderly
inmates based on comparisons with their younger counterparts is

constructed. Major areas of analysis include: personal characteristics,
current offense and sentence, probation and incarceration history,
conformity to prison rules, prison recreation and work activities, and
interaction with family members and friends outside of prison.
Recommendations for future investigation are included. A most thorough
review of the literature is provided. Excellent reference source.

326. Goetting, A. (1983). The elderly in prison: issues and
      perspectives. Journal of Research in Crime and Delinquency,
      July, 291-309.

This article is an in-depth overview of all areas pertinent to the older
prisoner. Research studies relevant to the demographical profile of the
prisoner, the prison environments, its social-psychological effects, the
interaction networks and status, conformity to rules, prison's effect on
social institution participation, the issue of parole, and the
availability of special prison policies, and facilities are discussed.
Because of methodological problems with sampling size and lack of
control groups, the research in all of these areas presents mixed
results. A nation-wide comprehensive survey of older prisoners is
advocated for humanitarian and legal reasons.

327. Ham, J. N. (1980). Aged and infirm male prison inmates. Aging,
      July-August, 24-31.

This study provides an evaluation of the conditions of confinement at
the Limited Duty Unit at the Columbus Correctional Facility, as they
affected aged, aged-infirm, and young-infirm male prison inmates. Data
for this evaluation study was collected from interviews with staff from
the correctional site, records, tours of various buildings, and from
interviews and observation of inmates. Special topics discussed
include: habitable floor space, bathrooms, food service, medical,
nutritional, rehabilitative and recreational services, fire protection,
neurosis, treatment and care, and activites. The article concludes with
the proposed legal action which charged that conditions of confinement
at the Prison's Limited Duty Unit were such that it led to an
acceleration of the debilitative processes associated with normal aging.
Important implications for social policy are inluded.

328. Ham, J. N. (1976). Forgotten minority: an exploration of
      long-term institutionalized aged and aging male prison inmates.
      Unpublished Dissertation, University of Michigan, Ann Harbor,
      Michigan.

There is an extensive study of the attitudes and life styles of aged and
aging inmates in a correctional institution in Jackson, Michigan. The
effects of institutional variations on the individual inmate were
measured in terms of their effects on the inmate's physical condition,
mental status, and social activity patterns within the institution.
These variables were selected to evaluate the total well being of the
inmate, measure the differential impact of institutional setting
characteristics on each area of functioning, and measure whether decline
in one area of functioning preceded or was related to decline in other
areas of functioning. Data was collected from interviews with staff,
institutional records, and from interviews and observations of the
inmate. The questionnaire and bibliography are included.

329.   Jensen, G. F. (1977). Age and rule breaking in prison: a test
       of sociocultural interpretations. Criminology, 14: 555-568.

This paper examines the relationship between age and rule-breaking in
prison from a sociological viewpoint. This study lends support to the
sociological positions on such differences by both specifying and
decomposing the age rule-breaking relationship. This study has also
attempted to test the applicability of sociological explanations to age
differences in rule violations among women in prison. Thus, despite the
limitations of this analysis for generalizing about and rule-breaking,
the results should reinforce faith in sociological interpretations of
differences which are often explained away in a non-sociological style.

330.   Johnson, R. (1982). Life under sentence of death. In R. Johnson
       & H. Toch (Eds.), The Pains of Imprisonment. Beverly Hills,
       California: Sage Publications.

Based on 35 open-ended interviews with inmates serving on death row in
Alabama, this chapter focuses on the dominent problems and pressures of
confinement as experienced by the prisoners. The author stresses the
fact some grow old prematurely and many describe themselves as "the
living dead." Significant differences were found between younger and
older prisoners. Older prisoners tended to have a more positive view of
death row and consequently expressed a lower degree of anxiety. While
older prisoners seem to benefit from their years of experience and
cumulated maturity, they felt more isolated from the prisoner and the
world at large.

331.   Krajick, K. (1979). Growing old in prison. Corrections
       Magazine, 5(1), 32-46.

This article gives an overview of the elderly in prison, who constitute
a minority of the prison population. Based on data from New York,
Michigan, and North Carolina, the special problems of elderly prisoners
are presented. These older offenders are usually first-time offenders,
have been convicted of a violent crime and are usually heavy users of
alcohol. Many are beginning to suffer the chronic health problems of
old age and are afraid of being victimized by younger, stronger inmates.
There are few prison systems with specific facilities for older
prisoners. Prison programs in four states, and project 60, a release
program, are discussed with regard to treatment of the elderly prisoner.
Several brief case studies are presented.

332.   MacKenzie, D. L. & Goodstein, L. (1985). Long-term incarceration
       impacts and characteristics of long-term offenders: an empirical
       analysis. Criminal Justice and Behavior, 12(4), 395-412.

This research examines various stress responses to imprisonment among
long and short-term inmates. The data used in this study was based on a
sample of 1,270 in three prisons: Stateville Correctional Center,
Illinois; Somers Correctional Institution, Connecticut; and Stillwater
Correctional Facility, Minnesota. Inmates new to prison, who
anticipated serving long terms, reported higher levels of stress and
lower self-esteem than did inmates who had already completed long prison

terms.   Short-term inmates new to prison reported less depression and
fewer psychosomatic illnesses compared to new inmates with long
sentences.   Distinct subgroup of long-term offenders (lifers versus
habituals) could be identified on the basis of demographic and past
history.

333.   Miller, D. T.   (1984).   Profile of inmates in the Texas
       Department of Corrections 60 years of age and older as of
       May 31, 1984. Texas Department of Corrections, Huntsville,
       Texas.

A brief report that provides a statistical profile of the 273 prisoners
who were at least 60 years old in the Texas Department of Corrections.
The typical geriatric prisoner was white, male 60-62 years of age,
protestant, and either married or divorced.   He had an education
achievement test score between 2.0 and 2.9, and an intelligence quotient
of 70-79.   The typical elderly prisoner had been convicted of one
offense, usually a homicide, in a metropolitan area.   He would be
considered a late life offender since he had received one or no adult
probated sentences prior to incarceration.   Generally, most offenders
had not been previously confined in a reformatory or any other prison.
The typical sentence was between 2 to 10 years and life.   Tables and
references are provided.

334.   Moore, E. O. (1985).   Prison environments and their impact
       on older prisoners.   Unpublished paper.   Department of
       Architecture, University of Nebraska, Lincoln, Nebraska.

This research presents the increasing problems that many municipal jails
and state and federal prisons face in housing older offenders.   Through
the use of structured in-depth interviews, 41 prisoners, who were 50
years or older and incarcerated in the Michigan Correctional Stystem,
were profiled.   Included in this analysis was a review of their health
problems as well as their general needs and problems unique to being an
aging prisoner.   This study also revealed a high level of fear of these
older prisoners when housed with younger inmates, often resulting in
reduced social interaction.   The reduction of aggressive behavior among
this group of older prisoners suggests a different management strategy
should be developed for older prisoners.   Important social policy
implications are addressed.

335.   Panton, J. H.   (1976).   Personality characteristics of aged
       inmates within a state prison population.   Offender
       Rehabilitation, 1(2), 203-208.

This study examined whether personality characteristics of aged male
inmates over the age of 60 are different in any way from those of the
general prison population.   The sample consisted of 120 aged inmates and
a representative population sample of 2,551 male inmates in North
Carolina.   An analysis of the Minnesota Multiphasic Personality
Inventory (MMPI) between the two groups formed the basis of this study.
The mean test profiles of both groups were indicative of a behavior
disorder, with the aged inmates presenting more neurotic and less
physchopathic responses than shown by the total inmate population.   This
lesser psychopathy implies for the aged inmate less antisocial
hostility.   It is concluded that the probability of receiving benefit

from psychotherapy or counseling appears to be more favorable for the aged inmates. References are provided.

336.   Mabli, J. & Patrick, J. (1979). Age and prison violence: increasing age heterogeneity as a violence-reducing strategy in prisons. Criminal Justice and Behavior, 6(2), 175-186.

This research describes a longitudinal project whereby older prisoners were transferred into the Federal Correctional Institution in El Reno, Oklahoma, and younger inmates into the Federal Correctional Institution in Texarkana, Arkansas, to reduce the violence at El Reno. The authors cite the important role that older prisoners have in reducing violence in a particular conflictive environment, since it was found that older prisoners had stabilized the situation. Several charts, statistical techniques, and references are provided.

337.   Reed, M. B. (1976). Aging in a total institution: the case of older prisoners. Unpublished Thesis, Middle Tennessee State University.

This study provides an overview of the social and cultural experiences of aging in prison. Respondents of the study were taken from the population of a major prison in Tennessee. They include all inmates over 50 years of age who had spent at least 10 years in prison. The sample consisted of 19 inmates who participated in a structured interview covering the following topics: information about family relations and friends, attitudinal items on religion and politics, and life events. Findings indicate that family relations are virtually nonexistent, however, the family is still considered an important symbol in the lives of the elderly. The author found that most elderly are interested in life, politics, and religion and most work in order to stay busy. Tables, a bibliography, and an appendix including the survey questionnaire is included.

338.   Rubenstein, D. (1984). The elderly in prison: a review of the literature. In E. S. Newman, D. J. Newman, M. L. Gewirtz, (Eds.), Elderly Criminals. Cambridge, MA: Oelgeschlager, Gunn & Hain, Publishers, Inc.

Using existing resources, this article attempts to identify the number of elderly prisoners (over the age of 50) as well as the types of crime that have brought them to prison. Two distinctive types of elderly prisoners are distinguished: chronic offenders and first-time prisoners. The problems in establishing a comprehensive profile of an elderly prisoner due to contradictory findings is presented. The psychological and sociological impact of prison life is thoroughly addressed. The chapter also includes some discussion of age integration versus age segregation prison environments. Methodological limitations are comprehensively outlined. Implications for future research to overcome current voids are also included.

339.   Teller, F. E. (1979). Criminal and psychological characteristics of the older prisoner . Unpublished Dissertation, University of Utah, Salt Lake City, Utah.

Utilizing prisoners over the age of fifty, a study was conducted to

determine the criminal and psychological characteristics. Comparisons
were made between older and younger male inmates as well as first
offenders and recidivists for both age groups. Records showing
demographic, psychological, and criminal variables were examined for 92
older inmates at the Utah State Prison. Of this sample, 37 percent were
first offenders and 63 percent were classified as recidivists. It was
concluded that older inmates had committed more crimes against persons
but fewer property crimes. The older prisoners also reported less
psychic pain and depression and were less socially deviant, impulsive,
and hostile. Late offenders were found to have engaged more often in
crimes of violence and were the best adjusted of all the inmates. A
bibliography, tables, and survey instrument are provided.

340. Tobin, P., & Metzler, C. (1983). Typology of older prisoners
      in Massachusetts State Correctional Facilities, 1972-1982.
      Unpublished Paper, Massachusetts Department of Corrections,
      Boston, MA.

A profile of prisoners over the age of 60 housed in Massachusetts State
Correctional Facilities included: the first offender, the chronic
offender, the prison recidivist, and the inmate grown old. Information
on admissions, releases, and the resident population at the beginning of
each year formed the basis for deriving the sample population. The four
types of older inmates appear dissimilar in the areas of offense
patterns, criminal history, and types of movement within the prison
system. The study suggests that a fourfold typology would be more
useful than the traditional dichotomous typology of elderly first
offender versus elderly recidivist. Tabular data and references are
provided.

341. Walter, B. L. (1980). A description of the elderly offender
      in Pennsylvania. Unpublished Dissertation, University of
      Pittsburg.

This study describes and analyzes the entire elderly offender population
in Pennsylvania's State Correctional System beginning September, 1973
through December, 1979. The offenders typically came from large
two-parent households, were predominantly middle children, were
non-abused and described their childhoods as positive experiences. The
elderly prison population described in this study was uneducated,
unskilled and possessed low level intellectual ability. There was found
to be a high incidence of alcoholism and unstable relationships. A
distinct connection was found between types of crimes and recidivism,
age at commitment and pattern of commitment. In terms of age at
commitment, the author found two distinct groups of prisoners with their
own unique characteristics. These two groups included young adult
offenders and geriatric delinquents. This study provides a
comprehensive comparison of these groups. Tables, references, and
survey instruments are included.

342. Washington, P. (1985). Mentally ill elderly offenders in five
      California county jails. Unpublished Paper. Department of
      Minority Studies, Wichita State University.

Demographic information on mentally ill men or mentally disordered
offenders in five California county jails is presented in this study.
Based upon a random sample of the entire jail population, respondents

for this study represents 65 older offenders who were 50 years of age or older. Of this group, 21 percent of those 50 years or older were diagnosed as mentally ill. Comparsions of the demographics of the mentally disordered offenders and non-mentally disordered offenders provides evidence of important differences between these two groups of elderly offenders. This study is unique in that it is one of the few attempts to investigate the extent of mental illness among the elderly in county jails.

343. Wiltz, C. J. (1978). Influence of age on length of
      incarceration. Unpublished Dissertation, University of Iowa.

Utilizing data from the Iowa Correctional System, this study provides an analysis of the role age plays on length of incarceration. The major hypothesis tested is whether older prison inmates will spend less time in prison than younger inmates. The sample included 1,700 inmates at the Iowa State Penitentiary. Aged inmates were defined as those 55 or over when they entered and left prison. To test the hypothesis, two other age groups (31 to 54) and those age 30 or less were included. A comprehensive profile is also presented for the sample on such topics as major disciplinary reports, prior prison commitments, length of sentence, type of offense, and inmate's physical condition. Aged inmates have no significant advantage over nonaged inmates and may not be perceived as less dangerous than nonaged inmates. Statistical tables and an extensive bibliography are included.

344. Wiltz, C. J. (1973). The aged prisoner: a case study of age
      and aging in prison. Unpublished Thesis, Kansas State
      University.

Based on a sample of 63 prisoners over the age of 60, the major research objectives of this study is to determine to what extent does age-grading exist in the institution, and to acquire some knowledge about how aging occurs in a prison setting. Issues related to age-grading among the older inmates were limited to the areas of friendship choices and their occupational roles. The major focus for these topics included: trustworthiness, mutual aid, intimacy in terms of conversation content, enactment of appropriate behavior, similar jobs, similar towns or coming into the institution together. In addition to addressing these major questions, the author provides a useful theoretical review of the literature focusing on prisonization.

345. Wooden, W. S. & Parker, J. (1980). Aged men in a prison
      environment: life satisfaction and coping strategies.
      Unpublished Paper. Department of Sociology, California State
      University, Long Beach, CA.

Case studies and interviews of 12 male prisoners between the ages of 50 and 64 residing in a medium security prison in California were conducted to determine attitudes of life satisfaction and examples of coping strategies in an institutional setting. Other issues explored included the role of the convict subculture and sexual code as it related to prison life for the older prisoner. Life satisfaction measures were based on self-reports of satisfaction including a discussion of social support systems that had developed within the prison groups. Various coping strategies such as maturity, family support, and positive outlook were mentioned.

346.   Vito, G.S F., & Wilson, D. G.   (1985).   Forgotten people:
       elderly inmates.   Federal Probation, 49(1), 18-24.

The article describes elderly inmates as a growing constituency with
special needs and problems. The authors categorize these problems and
special needs into five major areas: (1) adjustment to imprisonment, (2)
vulnerability to victimization, (3) adaptation to physical conditions,
(4) lack of suitable programs, and (5) diversity of the elderly inmate
population. It is suggested that the usual crisis management approach
in corrections will not solve the problem. Social policy issues are
discussed in detail.

347.   Wormer, V. K. (1981). To be old and in prison. In S. Letman,
       L. French, H. Scott, Jr., & D. Weichman (Eds.),   Contemporary
       Issues in Corrections. Jonesboro, Tennessee: Pilgrimage, Inc.

Based on a review of the literature, this chapter explores the social
psychological process of aging in prison. This approach is based on the
premise that the aging prisoner represents a very special population
with special needs and concerns. And because of these qualities aging
prisoners are forced to acquire coping strategies for a strange and
unusual situation at a time when coping mechanisms are diminished.
Specific topics focus on biological, psychological, and social
functioning and the aged inmate is reviewed in terms of the immediate
surroundings of prison. The concept of the total institution and its
impact on the aging prisoner in terms of psychological isolation,
health, isolation from family and friends, and a sense of agelessness
unique to the prison experience are discussed. The author provides a
very personal view of growing old in prison. References and important
implications for social policy are provided.

10 REHABILITATIVE PROGRAMS

348. Aday, R. H. (1977). Toward the development of a therapeutic program for older prisoners. Offender Rehabilitation, 1(4), Summer, 343-348.

A brief overview is given of the elderly offender and characteristics of institutional settings, both therapeutic and in general. The main body of the article describes a geriatric program in an Oklahoma prison. The program's effectiveness is measured by the prisoners' scores on the Life Satisfaction Index, which approximate the scores of a normal, non-institutionalized population. The importance of dealing therapeutically with elderly offenders is emphasized. Various innovative programs are described. References are provided.

349. Booth, D. (1985). Health status of the incarcerated elderly. Unpublished Paper. Department of Community Health, Wayne State University.

Stresses the need to recognize and support the need for special programs for the aging inmate. The age-related changes, and the maintenance of health and well being of elderly prisoners require special manangement skills/programs. Information is needed to develop proper programs in nutrition, exercise, and education that will maintain and promote the health of the elderly prisoners. The author feels that protection and promotion of the health of the elderly is likely to serve as a cost-containment measure for the criminal justice system, as well as enhance the overall quality of life for the elderly prisoner. Suggestions have important implications for policy decisions.

350. Cordilia, A. (1985). Older 'longtermers': patterns of re-entry after release from prison. Unpublished Paper. Department of Sociology, University of Massachusetts - Habor Campus.

This paper is based on in-depth interviews with 32 inmates before and after release from prisons. It focuses on the plans and expectations of life on the outside, as well as the actual post release experiences, which are characteristic of older ex-offenders who have served long prison terms. Their experiences are contrasted with those of younger ex-inmates as well as of ex-inmates who have served shorter sentences. The author suggests that older long term prisoners have counselling and other special needs whch are somewhat different from the more typical prisoner. References are included.

351. Fry, L. (1984). The implications of diversion for older
      offenders. In W. Wilbanks, & P. K. Kim, (Eds.), Elderly
      Criminals. New York: University Press.

This research is a description of a case study of a single California
County Adult Diversion Project which accepted a high percentage of older
persons. The purpose is to assess the implications of diversion and
other alternative processing programs for elderly offenders. A profile
of characteristics of older offenders ranging in age from 50 to 89 is
provided. While the project is considered a success, only offenders
charged with misdemeanor property crimes, victimless sex offenses, and
less serious public disturbances such as family dispute offenses were
included in the sample.

352. Feinberg, G., Glugover, S., & Zwetchkenbaum, I. (1984). The
      Broward senior intervention and education program: a pilot
      program. In E. S. Newman, D. J. Newman, & M. L. Gewirtz,
      (Eds.), Elderly Criminals. Cambridge, MA: Oelgeschlager, Gunn
      & Hain, Publishers, Inc.

The authors describe the Broward County Senior Intervention Education
Program (BSIE) founded in April, 1979. The program is designed for
elderly offenders, 60 years of age or older who have been arrested and
have appeared before the courts for misdemeanor shoplifting. The major
objective of this chapter is to present the important components of the
program including the various stages of offender treatment. The chapter
provides a special assessment of the elderly shoplifter which tends to
show them in a different light when compared to shoplifters from other
age categories. Evaluation procedures for such a program are also
discussed. Important policy implications are discussed.

353. Feinberg, G. (1983). Shoplifting by the elderly: one
      community's innovative response. Aging, Oct-Nov., 20-24.

An overview is provided concerning the increased tendency for the
elderly to be involved in the criminal justice system. In particular
the crime of shoplifting among the elderly is reviewed. Several
theories are discussed as to why the elderly turn to shoplifting late in
life. Special strategies are introduced for dealing with shoplifting by
the elderly. The Broward County Program in Florida is reviewed. Social
policy issues are integrated throughout the article.

354. Gewirtz, M. L. (1984). Social work practice with elderly
      offenders. In E. S. Newman, D. J. Newman, M. L. Gewirtz,
      (Eds.), Elderly Criminals. Cambridge, MA: Oelgeschlager,
      Gunn & Hain, Publishers, Inc.

The author fuses theoretical knowledge with practice skills from two
fields, social work and gerontology. The major focus is to develop an
intervention strategy for working specifically with elderly populations.
This approach presents a modified version of the Integrative Approach
for gerontological practice based on the work of Edmund Sherman.

Application and limitations of the approach in working with elderly offenders are explored, and issues for additional research and clarification are recommended. Questions are raised regarding the possibility of developing a separate criminal justice system for the elderly as their numbers swell in the future. Conclusions focus on important consideration for social policy.

355. Glugover, S. & Zwetchkenbaum, I. (1986). Community alternatives to arrest in shoplifting cases: a pilot program. Boward Senior Intervention and Education Program, Southeast Focal Point Senior Center, Hollywood, Florida.

This paper describes a special program designed especially for older offenders in the criminal justice system. Special strategies for working with the elderly which require both remedial and preventive components are described. Goals for the pilot program are thoroughly outlined which include counseling, rehabilitative services and criminal justice alternatives especially designed for elderly clients. Barriers which have hindered the development of the program are noted.

356. Goetting, A. (1984). Prison programs and facilities for elderly inmates. In E. S. Newman, D. J. Newman, & M. L. Gewirtz, (Eds.), Elderly Criminals. Cambridge, MA: Oelgeschlager, Gunn & Hain, Publishers, Inc.

This chapter describes the existence of special policies, programs, and facilities in the United States. Only three states offered Aged Offender Programs. It is concluded that programs or facilities based on age are rare. Policy recommendations centering around the special needs of institutionalized senior citizens are outlined. Questions are raised concerning current prison policies which need further research attention. Several theoretical explanations for elderly criminal behavior is also included.

357. Johnson, E. (1985). Care for elderly inmates: what can the prison do? Unpublished Paper. Center for the Study of Crime, Delinquency and Corrections. Southern Illinois University.

This paper is a theoretical attempt to address the important issues facing the criminal justice system where the aging prisoner is concerned. Although the elderly account for a small portion of persons arrested and imprisoned, the author stresses the all types of institutions (nursing homes, boarding homes, mental hospitals, and prisons) should meet standards for physical and emotional security, safeguards against fire, medical care, securiy of belongings, good nutrition, constructive leisure and a proper emotional atmosphere. However, it is concluded that only recently that the criminal justice has begun to address the special needs of the elderly population.

358. Malley, A. (1981). The advocate program sees the elderly through. The Florida Bar Journal, March 1981.

A descriptive article that describes the unique personal, social, legal and economic needs of persons 60 years and older who become involved with the criminal justice system. Eight elaborate goals surrounding the Advocate Seniors Program which was launched in 1978 is provided.

Possible explanations for the elderly's antisocial and criminal activities are discussed. Examples of client involvement and program success are included.

359. Markham, G. R. (1981). Community service for elderly offenders. Police Journal, 54(3), 235-238.

This brief article describes a special program which takes into consideration the elderly offender's medical and social status before a referral decision is made. At the time an elderly person is arrested or reported for a criminal offense, the police notifies the appropriate social service division, which assessed the seriousness of the offense and the circumstances of the accused. Referral to any agency or person is done only with the knowledge and consent of the elderly person. Case examples are provided.

360. McCarthy, B. R. & Lamgworthy, R. H. (1985). Older offenders on probation and parole. Unpublished Paper, Criminal Justice Department, University of Alabama at Birmingham.

This descriptive paper presents a profile of a sample of 95 older felons under community supervision. This group is the single largest group of older convicted offenders, outnumbering prisoners by four to one. The comprehensive profile includes descriptions of personal data, criminal history, type of offense and supervision success. Comparisons are made between the processing of women and older offenders in the criminal justice system. This particular discussion focuses on discrimination, leniency and neglect. Five tables and an extensive bibliography is provided.

361. Rideau, W., & Sinclair, B. (1982). Growing old in prison. Angolite, 7(4), 33-40.

This article describes a special program developed at the Louisiana State Penitentiary. For prisoners who are too old to care for themselves in the regular prison population, a special nurse-care unit for elderly prisoners was developed. This program was initiated due to the increasing number of lifers (over 1,000), many of which are old or becoming old. Special activities of the program are described. Case examples and photographs are included.

III RESOURCES AND INFORMATION

A. Crime Prevention Programs For Older Persons

Interagency Task Force on Crime
    Against the Elderly
Los Angeles County Department of
    Senior Citizens Affairs
601 South Kingsley Drive
Los Angeles, CA 90005
(213) 385-4221

Prevention-Crimes Against the
    Elderly
Office of the Attorney General
Crime Prevention Unit
3580 Wilshire Boulevard, Suite 938
Los Angeles, CA 90010
(213) 620-3286

Elderly Victims of Crime
Santa Cruz County Sheriff Office
    Of Corrections
P.O. Box 623
Santa Cruz, CA 95016

Elderly Street Victims
Wilmington Crime Resistance Task
    Force
Federal Bureau of Investigation
P.O. Box 1872
Wilmington, DE 19899

Crime Prevention Program
NRTA/AARP
1909 K Street NW
Washington, DC 20049

Crimes Against the Elderly
Sarasota City Police Department
P.O. Box 3528
Sarasota, FL 33578
(813) 366-8000

Locks for the Elderly
Office of Crime Prevention
1510 First Avenue North
St. Petersburg, FL 33705
(813) 893-7623

Project Concern
City of St. Petersburg
1510 First Avenue North
St. Petersburg, FL 33705
(813) 893-7623

Senior Citizen Lock Project
South Bend Police Department
701 West Sample Street
South Bend, IN 46625
(219) 284-9265

Crime Prevention for Seniors
Louisville Division of Police
633 West Jefferson Street
(502) 581-2569

Citizen Involvement Program
Council on Criminal Justice
26 S. Calvert Street, Room 101
Baltimore, MD 21202

Crime Prevention Program for
    the Elderly
Mayor's Office of Baltimore City
26 S. Calvert Street, Room 1101
Baltimore, MD 21202
(301) 396-4370

Crime Cautions for Seniors
Minneapolis Police Department
Room 130, City Hall
Minneapolis, MN 55415
(612) 348-6870

Aid To Elderly Victims of Crime
Mid-America Regional Council
20 West 9th Street
Kansas City, MO 64105
(816) 474-4240

Victimization of Elderly
New York City Department of the
    Aging
250 Broadway
New York, NY 10007
(21) 566-0154

Volunteer Crime Prevention
Cottage Grove Police Department
28 South 6th Street
Cottage Grove, OR 97242

Older Seniors' Crime Prevention
Multnomah County Division of
    Public Safety
10525 SE Cherry Blossom Drive
Portland, OR 97216
(503) 255-1891

Elderly Crime Reporting Program
Center for Studies in Aging
North Texas State University
Denton, TX 76203
(817) 565-2296

Operations Lifeline
Huntington Police Department
Crime Prevention Unit
Huntington, WV 25717
(304) 696-5575

Neighborhood Security Aide
    Program
Courthouse, Room 1
901 North 9th Street
Milwaukee, WI 53233
(414) 278-5021

B. State Agencies on Aging

Alabama
Helen Geesey, Director
Commission on Aging
State Capitol
Montgomery, Alabama 36130
205/261-5743

Alaska
Jon B. Wolfe, Executive Director
State of Alaska
Older Alaskans Commission
Pouch C. M.S. 0209
Juneau, Alaska 99811
907/465-3250

Arizona
Douglas X. Patimo, Director
Aging and Adult Administration
1400 West Washington Street
Phoenix, Arizona 85005
602/266-4448

Arkansas
Randall A. McCain, Director
Arkansas Office on Aging
Donaghey Building - Suite 1428
7th and Main Streets
Little Rock, Arkansas
501/371-2441

California
Alice Gonzales, Director
Department of Aging
1020 19th Street
Sacramento, California 95814
916/322-5290

Colorado
William J. Hanna, Director
Aging and Adult Services
Department of Social Services
717 7th St - Box 181000
Denver, Colorado 80218-0899
303/294-5913

Connecticut
Mary Klinek, Director
Department on Aging
175 Main Street
Hartford, Connecticut 06106
203/566-7725

Delaware
Eleanor Cain, Director
Division on Aging
Department of Health & Social
    Services
1901 N. Dupont Highway
New Castle, Delaware 19720
302/421-6791

District of Columbia
E. Veronica Pace, Director
District of Columbia
    Office on Aging
1412 K Street, N.W.
Second Floor
Washington, D.C. 20005
202/724-5622

Florida
John Stokesberry, Director
Program Office of Aging
Department of Health and
    Rehabilitation Services
1317 Winewood Blvd.
Tallahassee, Florida 32301
904/488-8922

Georgia
Randy Oven, Director
Office of Aging
Department of Human Resources
878 Peachtree St. N.E., Room 632
Atlanta, Georga 30309
904/488-8922

Hawaii
Renji Gota, Director
Executive Office on Aging
Office of the Governor
335 Merchant St., Room 241
Honolulu, Hawaii 96813
808/548-2593

Idaho
Gary H. Gould, Director
Idaho Office on Aging
Statehouse - Room 114
Boise, Idaho 83720
208/334-3833

Illinois
Peg R. Blaser, Director
Department on Aging
421 East Capitol Avenue
Springfield, Illinois 62706
217/785-3356

Indiana
Jean Merritt, Executive Director
Department on Aging & Community
    Services
115 N. Penn Street - Suite 1350
Indianapolis, Indiana 46204
317/232-7006

Iowa
Karen L. Tynes, Director
Commission on Aging
914 Grand Ave.
Jewett Building
Des Moines, Iowa 50319
515/281-5187

Kansas
Sylvia Hougland, Director
Department on Aging
610 West 10th Street
Topeka, Kansas 66612
913/296-4986

Kentucky
Peggy T. Mooney, Director
Division for Aging Services
Bureau of Social Services
275 East Main Street
Frankfort, Kentucky
502/564-6930

Louisiana
Margaret W. Sloan, Director
Office of Elderly Affairs
P.O. Box 80374
Capitol Station
Baton Rouge, Louisiana 70898
504/925-17000

Maine
Patricia Riley, Director
Bureau of Maine's Elderly
Department of Human Services
State House, Station 11
Augusta, Maine 04333
207/289-2561

Maryland
Matthew Tayback, Director
Office on Aging
State Office Building
301 West Preston Street
Baltimore, Maryland 21201
301/225-1100

Massachusetts
Richard H. Rowland, Secretary
Department of Elder Affairs
38 Chauncy Street
Boston, Massachusetts 02111
617/727-7751

Michigan
Kenneth Oettle, Director
Office of Services to the Aging
300 East Michigan
P.O. box 30026
Lansing, Michigan 48909
517/373-8230

Minnesota
Gerald A. Bloedow, Director
Metro Square Bldg., Room 204
7th and Robert Street
St. Paul, Minnesota 55101
612/296-2544

Mississippi
Jay Moon, Executive Director
Mississippi Council on Aging
301 West Pearl St.
Jackson, Mississippi
601/949-2070

Missouri
Rick Westpal, Director
Office on Aging
Department of Social Services
Broadway State Office Building
P.O. Box 570
Jefferson City, Missouri
314/751-3082

Montana
Norma Vestre, Administrator
Commuity Services Division
Department of Social Services
P.O. Box 4210
Helena, Montana 59604
406/449-3865

Nebraska
Heather N. Hong, Director
Department on Aging
P.O. Box 85044
301 Centennial Mall South
Lincoln, Nebraska 68509
402/471-2306

Nevada
S. Barton Jacka, Director
Division of Aging Services
Department of Human Resources
505 E. King Street, Room 600
KinKead Building
Carson City, Nevada 89710
702/885-4210

New Hampshire
Stephanie Eaton, Director
Council on Aging
105 London Rd., Bldg. 3
Concord, New Hampshire 03301
603/271-2751

New Jersey
Jacques O. Lebel, Director
Department of Community Affairs
P.O. Box 2768
363 West State Street
Trenton, New Jersey
609/292-4833

New Mexico
Eugene, T. Varela, Administrator
State Agency on Aging
LaVilla Rivera Building
224 East Palace Avenue
Santa Fe, New Mexico 87501
505/827-7640

New York
Eugene S. Callender, Director
N.Y. State Office for the Aging
Agency Building 2
Empire State Plaza
Albany, New York 12223
518/474-5731

North Carolina
Ernest B. Messer, Director
Division on Aging
Department of Human Resources
708 Hillsborough St.
Raleigh, North Carolina
919/733-3983

North Dakota
Larry Brewster, Administrator
State Agency on Aging
Department of Human Services
State Capitol Building
Bismarck, North Dakota 58505
701/224-2577

Ohio
Joyce F. Chapple, Director
Commission on Aging
50 West Broad Street
Columbus, Ohio 43215
614/466-5500

Oklahoma
Roy R. Keen, Administrator
Special Unit on Aging
Department of Human Services
P.O. Box 25352
Oklahoma City, Oklahoma 73125
405/521-2281

Oregon
Richard C. Ladd, Administrator
Senior Services Division
Human Resources Department
Room 313
Public Services Building
Salem, Oregon 97301
503/378-4728

Pennsylvania
Jacqueline L. Nowak, Director
Department of Aging
231 State St.
Harrisburg, Pennsylvania 17101
717/783-1550

Rhode Island
Anna M. Tucker, Director
Department of Elderly Affairs
79 Washington Street
Providence, Rhode Island 02903
401/277-2858

South Carolina
Harry R. Bryan, Director
Commission on Aging
915 Main Street
Columbia, South Carolina 29201
803/758-2576

South Dakota
Michael Vogel, Administrator
Adult Services & Aging
Division of Human Development
Richard F. Dreip Building
700 N. Illinois Street
Pierre, South Dakota 57501
605/773-3656

Tennessee
Emily M. Wiseman, Director
Commission on Aging
703 Tennessee Building
535 Church Street
Nashville, Tennessee 37219
615/741-2056

Texas
Chris Kyker, Director
Department of Aging
P.O. Box 12786
Capitol Station
Austin, Texas 78711
512/475-2717

Utah
Louise Lintz
APS Program Specialist
Division of Aging Services
150 West North Temple
Room 326
Salt Lake city, Utah 84103
801/533-6422

Vermont
Mary Ellen Spencer, Director
Office on the Aging
103 Main Street
Waterbury, Vermont 05676
802/241-2400

Virginia
Wilda Ferguson, Director
Office on Aging
101 North 14th St.
James Monroe Bldg., 18th Floor
Richmond, Virginia 23219
804/225-2271

Washington
Charles Reed, Director
Bureau of Aging and Adult
    Services

Department of Social and Health
    Services, OB-43G
Olympia, Washington
206/753-2502

West Virginia
Phillip D. Turner, Director
West Virginia Commission
    On Aging
State Capital
Charleston, West Viriginia 25305
303/348-3317

Wisconsin
Donna McDowell, Director
Department of Health and Social
    Services
1 West Wilson Street - Room 686
Madison, Wiconsin 53703
608/266-2536

Wyoming
Scott Sessions, Director
Commission on Aging

Department of Social Services
Hathaway Building - Room 139
Cheyenne, Wyoming 82002
307/777-7986

C. State Correction Agencies

Alabama
Morris L. Thigpen, Commissioner
Department of Corrections
101 S. Union Street
Montgomery, Alabama   36130
205/834-1227

Alaska
Susan Humphrey-Barnett, Director
Department of Corrections
2200 East 42nd Ave.
Anchorage, Alaska   99508-5202
907/561-4426

Arizona
Samuel A. Lewis, Director
Department of Corrections
1601 W. Jefferson
Phoenix, Arizona   85007
602/255-5536

Arkansas
A. L. Lockhart, Director
Department of Corrections
P.O. Box 8707
Pine Bluff, Arkansas 71611
501/247-1800

California
N.A. Chaderjian, Secretary
Youth & Adult Corrections
1100-11th Street, Fourth Floor
Sacramento, California   95814
916/323-6001

Colorado
W.L. Kautzky, Director
Department of Corrections
2862 S. Circle Dr., Suite #400
Colorado Springs, Colorado 80906
303/579-9580

Connecticut
Raymond M. Lopes, Commissioner
Department of Corrections
340 Capital Avenue
Hartford, Connecticut   06106
203/566-5710

Delaware
John L. Sullivan, Commissioner
Department of Corrections
80 Monrovia Ave.
Smyrna, Delaware   19977
302/736-5601

District of Columbia
Hallem H. Williams, Director
Department of Corrections
1923 Vermont Ave., N.W.
Washington, D.C. 20001
202/673-7316

Florida
Richard L. Dugger, Secretary
Department of Corrections
1311 Winewood Blvd.
Tallahassee, Florida 32399-2500
904/488-5021

Georgia
David C. Evans, Commissioner
Department of Corrections
2 Martin Luther King, Jr. Drive
Atlanta, Georgia 30334
404/656-4593

Hawaii
Winona E. Rubin, Director
Department of Social Services
P.O. Box 339
Honolulu, Hawaii 96809
808/548-6260

Illinois
Michael P. Lane, Director
Department of Corrections
P.O. Box 19277
Springfield, Illinois 62794-9277
217/522-2666

Indiana
John T. Shettle, Commissioner
Department of Corrections
804 State Office Building
Indianapolis, Indiana 46204
317/232-5766

Iowa
Harold Farrier, Director
Department of Corrections
Suite 250, 10th & Grand
Des Moines, Iowa 50309
515/281-4811

Kansas
Richard A. Mills, Secretary
Department of Corrections
Landon State Office Bldg.
900 Jackson, Suite 404-N
Topeka, Kansas 66612
913/296-3317

Kentucky
George W. Wilson, Secretary
Department of Corrections
State Office Building
Frankford, Kentucky 40601
502/564-4726

Louisiana
C. Paul Phelps, Secretary
Department of Corrections
P.O. Box 94303, Capital Station
Baton Rouge, Louisiana 70804
504/342-6740

Maine
Donald L. Allen, Commissioner
Department of Corrections
State House - Station #111
Augusta, Maine 04333
207/289-2711

Maryland
Arnold J. Hopkins, Commissioner
Division of Corrections
6776 Reisterstown Rd., Suite 309
Baltimore, Maryland 21215-2342
301/764-4100

Massachusetts
Michael V. Fair, Commissioner
Department of Corrections
100 Cambridge St.
Boston, Massachusetts
617/727-3301

Michigan
Robert Brown, Jr., Director
Department of Corrections
P.O. Box 30003
Lansing, Michigan 48909
517/373-0283

Minnesota
Orville B. Pung, Commissioner
Department of Corrections
300 Bigelow Bldg.
450 N. Syndicate St.
St. Paul, Minnesota 55104
612/642-0200

Mississippi
Donald Cabana, Commissioner
Department of Corrections
723 N. President St.
Jackson, Mississippi 39202
601/354-6454

Missouri
Dick D. Moore, Director
Department of Corrections
P.O. Box 236
Jefferson City, Missouri 65102
314/751-2389

Montana
Daniel D. Russell, Administrator
Department of Institutions
1539 11th Ave.
Helena, Montana 59620
406/444-5671

Nebraska
Frank O. Gunter, Director
Department of Corrections
P.O. Box 94661
Lincoln, Nebraska 68509-4661
402/471-2654

Nevada
George W. Sumner, Director
Department of Prisons
P.O. Box 7011
Carson City, Nevada 89702
402/471-2156

New Hampshire
Ronald L. Powell, Commissioner
Department of Corrections
P.O. Box 769
Concord, New Hampshire 03301
603/224-3500

New Jersey
William H. Fauver, Commissioner
Department of Corrections
CN-863
Trenton, New Jersey 08625
2609/292-9860

New Mexico
O.L. McCotter, Secretary
Department of Corrections
1422 Paseo de Peralta
Santa Fe, New Mexico 87501
505/827-8645

New York
Thomas Coughlin III, Commissioner
Department of Corrections
State Office Building Campus
Albany, New York 12226
518/457-8126

North Carolina
John G. Patseavouras, Director
Department of Corrections
831 W. Morgan Street
Raleigh, North Carolina 27603
919/733-3226

North Dakota
Elaine Little, Chief Officer
Director of Institutions
State Capitol
Bismarck, North Dakota 58505
701/224-2471

Ohio
Richard P. Seiter, Director
Department of Rehabilitation
1050 Freeway Drive North
Columbus, Ohio 43229
614/466-8965

Oklahoma
Larry R. Meachum, Director
Department of Corrections
P.O. Box 11400
Oklahoma City, Oklahoma 73136
405/427-6511

Oregon
Thomas G. Toombs, Administrator
Corrections Division
2575 Center Street, N.E.
Salem, Oregon 97310
503/378-2467

Pennsylvania
Glen R. Jeffes, Commissioner
Department of Corrections
Box 598
Camp Hill, Pennsylvania 17011
717/975-4860

Rhode Island
Jonh J. Moran, Director
Department of Corrections
75 Howard Avenue
Cranston, Rhode Island 02920
401/464-2611

South Carolina
W.D. Leeke, Commissioner
Department of Corrections
P.O. Box 21787
Columbia, South Carolina 29221
803/758-6321

South Dakota
Jim P. Smith, Executive Director
State Board of Corrections
523 E. Capital
Pierre, South Dakota 57501
605/773-3478

Tennessee
Stephen H. Norris, Commissioner
Department of Corrections
320 6th Avenue, North
Nashville, Tennessee 37219-5252
615/741-2071

Texas
Lane McCotter, Director
Department of Corrections
P.O. Box 99
Huntsville, Texas 77340
409/295-6371

Utah
Gary W. DeLand, Director
Department of Corrections
6100 S. 300 E., Suite 400
Salt Lank City, Utah 84107
801/264-2151

Vermont
Joseph J. Patrissi, Commissioner
Department of Corrections
103 S. Main Street
Waterbury, Vermont 05676
802/242-2263

Virginia
Edward W. Murray, Director
Department of Corrections
P.O. Box 26963
Richmond, Virginia 23261-6963
804/257-1900

Washington
Chase Riveland, Secretary
Department of Corrections
P.O. Box 9699
Olympia, Washington 98501
206/753-1573

West Virginia
A.V. Dodrill, Jr., Commissioner
Department of Corrections
112 California Ave., Room 300
Charleston, West Virginia 25305
304/348-2037

Wisconsin
Stephen Babitch, Administrator
Division of Corrections
P.O. Box 7925
Madison, Wisconsin 53707
608/266-2471

Wyoming
Donald L. Boyer, Administrator
State Board of Charities /Reform
Herscher Bldg.
Cheyenne, Wyoming 82002
307/777-7405

D. Groups and Organizations to Contact

AARP National Gerontology
   Resource Center
1909 K. St., NW
Washington, DC 20049
202/728-4700

American Civil Liberties Union
22 East 40th St.
New York, New York 10016
212/944-9800

American Correctional Association
4321 Hartwick Rd.
College Park, Maryland   20740
301/699-7600

American Geriatrics Society
Ten Columbus Circle
New York, New York 10019
212/582-13333

American Judicature Society
200 W. Monroe St., Suite 1606
Chicago, Illinois   60606
312/558-6900

American Justice Institute
725 University Ave.
Sacramento, California 95825
916/924-3700

Andrus Gerontological Information
  Center
University of Southern California
University Park
Los Angeles, California 90007
213/743-5990

American Society on Aging
833 Market St
Suite 516
San Francisco, California 94103
415/543-2617

Christic Institute
1324 Capitol St.
Washington, DC 20002
202/797-8106

Concerned Relatives of Nursing
  Home Patients
P.O. Box 11820
Cleveland, Ohio 44118
216/321-0403

Consumer Protection Center
2000 L Street, N.W.
Suite 307
Washington, DC 20052
202/676-7585

Contact Inc.
P.O. Box 81826
Lincoln, Nebraska 68501

Legal Research and Services For
  The Elderly
925 15th St., NW
Washington, DC 20005
202/347-8800

Legal Services for the Elderly
132 W. 43rd St., 3rd Floor
New York, New York 10036
212/595-1340

National Alliance of Senior
  Citizens
101 Park Washington Court
Suite 125
Falls Church, vikrginia 22046
702/241-1533

National citizens coalition for
  Nursing Home Reform
1309 L. St., NW
Washington, DC 20005
202/393-7979

National Institute of
  Victimology
2333 N. Vernon St.
Arlington, Virginia 22207
703/528-8872

National Organization for
  Victim Assistance
1757 Park Rd., NW
Washington, DC 20010
202/232-8560

National Senior Citizens Law
  Center
1636 W. 8th St., Suite 201
Los Angeles, California 90017
213/232-8560

SCAN
National Clearinghouse on Aging
300 Independence Ave., SW
Washington, DC 20201

Select Committee on Aging
House Annex #1, Room 712
Washington, DC 20515
202/226-5364

Special Committee on Aging
U.S. Senate Office Bldg.
Room G-233
Washington, DC 20515
202/225-5364

AUTHOR INDEX

Includes both authors and joint authors.
Numbers after each name refer to entry number.

SUBJECT INDEX

About the Author

RON H. ADAY is Associate Professor and Gerontology Program Coordinator at Middle Tennessee State University.